KNITS FOR HATS
GLOVES & SCARVES

The Craft Library

KNITS FOR HATS

GLOVES & SCARVES

20 original designs for everyone

Louisa Harding

hamlyn

An Hachette UK Company
www.hachette.co.uk

First published in Great Britain in 2005 by
Hamlyn, a division of Octopus Publishing Group Ltd
Endeavour House
189 Shaftesbury Avenue
London
WC2H 8JY
www.octopusbooks.co.uk

This edition published in 2013

ISBN: 978-0-600-62724-1

A CIP catalogue record for this book is available from the British Library

Printed and bound in China

10 9 8 7 6 5 4 3 2

contents

38

102

78

Introduction

There is something very comforting about being wrapped up against the winter elements. As a child you were told to wrap up warm, winding scarves round and round, pulling hats over ears and tugging on gloves or mittens on strings, hardly able to breathe with all the layers. Once outside and battling against a chill wind, kicking up autumn leaves or throwing snowballs, you felt grateful for all the fuss.

Now, as I get my family ready to venture out on frosty mornings, I too make them layer up. And it is with an added sense of satisfaction, knowing that the hats, gloves and scarves they are pulling on I have made for them, enveloping them in gorgeous yarns to keep them warm. With every handknitted stitch, I am passing on my affection and love.

The aim of this book is to offer a collection of desirable handknitted accessories. Whether you knit them for yourself or for your loved ones, I hope you will find a project to inspire you. I wanted the designs to be modern, stylish and fun; the patterns, easy, approachable and quick to knit. A simple knowledge of the most basic knitting skills is all you need to tackle the projects – the pom pom scarf on page 108 doesn't require you to pick up a knitting needle and makes an ideal project for the youngest enthusiast.

I have included some supremely practical designs, such as the beanie hat on page 68, with a version for every member of the family – the fun here is to customize, to suit each individual. There are also designs worked in beautiful, luxurious yarns: take a look at the delicate lacy scarf in silk and mohair on page 112, an indulgent treat if knitted for yourself, and the man's cashmere moss stitch scarf on page 122, the ideal gift for your beloved. I have added traditional extra-long ribbed scarves and funky tweedy gloves, while updated classics like the ribbed hat, stripy scarf and pretty mittens complete the collection.

Enjoy the knitting – and the wearing, wrapped up cosy and warm.

How to use this book

The projects in this book have been designed to appeal to a wide range of knitters, from those just picking up their needles for the first time to more experienced knitters looking for the ultimate hat, glove or scarf pattern. Many of the designs have two or more variations, and I have used a range of different knitted edgings, finishing details and embellishments to add interest and ensure that there is something for everyone!

Techniques

The basic knitting techniques used in the book are explained on pages 10–29. This chapter also includes information on yarns, how to knit from a chart, and a list of the abbreviations used in the patterns. Full instructions are provided on pressing your completed knitting and how to make up your project for a perfect finish. The following chapter (see pages 30–7) explains how to create pom poms, tassels, fringing and cords, plus an array of pretty knitted and embroidered motifs – all the little details that will give your project its unique look.

Using the patterns

Each pattern has written instructions that you should follow carefully; the Fairisle hat on page 64 also has a chart to work from (see page 28 for advice on knitting from a chart). Each part of the pattern is explained in the example shown here.

Each pattern is worked out mathematically, so if the correct tension is not achieved the item will not fit. Before you start knitting your project, check your tension as follows:

1 Using the needle size given in the pattern, cast on 5–10 more stitches than stated in the tension details and work 5–10 more rows.

2 When your tension square is complete, lay it on a flat surface, place a rule or tape measure horizontally across the knitting and count the number of stitches to 10 cm (4 in). This should equal the number of stitches stated in the tension given for the pattern.

3 Place the measure vertically and count the number of rows to 10 cm (4 in). This should equal the number of rows stated in the tension given for the pattern.

4 If you have too many stitches/rows to 10 cm (4 in), knit another tension square using a thicker needle and check again. If you have too few stitches/rows to 10 cm (4 in), do the same using a finer needle.

Some of the patterns are knitted in rib, textured pattern or with cables. It is difficult to measure the tension of these patterns as they are meant to have an elastic fit. The pattern will specify whether the tension swatch should be knitted in pattern or stocking stitch. Check your tension regularly as you knit your project.

Materials

Lists all the yarns needed, in the quantities required to complete your chosen project. More information on yarns is provided on page 26.

Details

Lists any other items (pom poms, tassels, etc.) needed to complete your chosen project. Instructions for making up these items are given on pages 30–7.

Needles

Lists the knitting needles used to make the project. The smaller needles are usually used for edgings or ribs, the larger needles for the main body fabric. You may need to change the size of needles used, depending on the tension of your knitting (see Tension).

Sizes

These are approximate, as the fit of the hats, gloves and scarves are all so different. For children's sizes, approximate ages are given. If you are unsure which size to choose, measure an existing item that fits well.

Tension

This is the single most important factor when you begin knitting. You will need to check your tension before you start knitting your project (see page 8).

Abbreviations

Lists all the abbreviations used in the pattern (see also page 29), and may

---

Winter warmer

Out for a walk on a snowy day, your outfit is not complete without a traditional ribbed hat. Add some fabulous pom poms and let the snowballs fly.

Materials

• Blue hat
Two 50 g (2 oz) balls of Jaeger Matchmaker Merino Aran in sky (770 Ice)
Pair of 4.5 mm (US 7) knitting needles
Two 4.5 cm (1¾ in) and five 3.5 cm (1¼ in) pom poms made using one 50 g (2 oz) ball of Jaeger Matchmaker Merino Aran in navy (629 Mariner)

• Camel hat
Two 50 g (2 oz) balls of Jaeger Matchmaker Merino Aran in camel (766 Soft Camel)
Pair of 4.5 mm (US 7) knitting needles
6.5 cm (2½ in) pom pom

Sizes
• Small (to fit child aged 5 upwards)
 46 cm (18 in) circumference
• Medium (to fit average adult female head)
 56 cm (22 in) circumference

Tension
24 sts x 26 rows to 10 cm (4 in) square measured over rib pattern using 4.5 mm (US 7) knitting needles

Abbreviations
dec decrease(e)(ing); **K** knit; **k2tog** knit 2 stitches together; **P** purl; **P2tog** purl 2 sts together; **RS** right side; **st(s)** stitch(es); **WS** wrong side

Designer's note
To use up oddments of yarn, this hat would also look really cute knitted in different-coloured stripes. The pom poms could then be worked in a range of sizes and colours.

Working instructions
Pattern is written for small size first with medium size in brackets.

hats **45**

---

include a special abbreviation applicable to that pattern only.

Designer's note

Includes tips and hints, comments on the design, yarn and detailing used, suggestions for variations and suitability for beginners.

Making instructions

Provides full instructions for knitting the pattern pieces.

Finishing instructions

Explains how to add the finishing details to your project.

techniques

and materials

The purpose of this chapter is to provide a beginner's guide to knitting. With a basic knowledge of the simplest stitches, and of the other techniques described here, you will be able to create your own hats, gloves and scarves using the patterns in this book.

Holding the needles

Before you cast on, get used to holding the yarn and the needles. They will feel awkward at first, but the more you try, the easier it will get. Don't forget to move your arms and your elbows when you knit, if you only move your wrists, you will find knitting really difficult.

Holding the right needle

1 The right needle is held in the same way as a pencil. When casting on and working the first few rows, the knitted piece rests between the thumb and the index finger. As the knitting grows, let the thumb slide under the knitted piece and hold the needle from below.

Holding the left needle

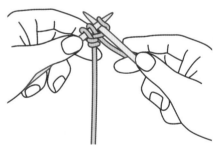

2 The left needle is held lightly over the top. The thumb and index finger control the tip of the needle

Holding the yarn

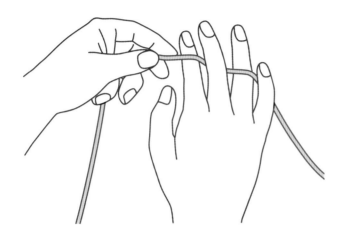

Holding the yarn

There are many ways of holding the yarn in the right hand. The way shown is the one most commonly used, but as you get more fluent, you will find the best method for you. The only thing you need to bear in mind is that the yarn needs to be able to move fluidly through your fingers and hand without getting tied up or caught, or the evenness of your knitting will suffer and you will never obtain the right tension.

Pass the yarn under your little finger, over your third finger, under your middle finger and over your index finger. The index finger is used to pass the yarn around the tip of the left needle when knitting. The tension and flow of the yarn is controlled by gripping the yarn in the crook of the little finger.

If you find it difficult to control the tension, then pass the yarn around the fingers in the same way, but pass it under and around the little finger before passing it over the third finger. The yarn circled around the little finger creates the tension to keep the knitting even.

Tip

It is important to relax when you are knitting. If you are tense and sitting uncomfortably, it will show in your knitting, however expert you become.

Casting on

This is the term used to describe making the first row of stitches, which forms the foundation for each piece of knitting. The 'cable cast-on' method shown here uses two needles and produces a firm, neat finish. It is very important that you achieve an even cast-on to avoid a wavy edge to your knitting, and this may require some practice.

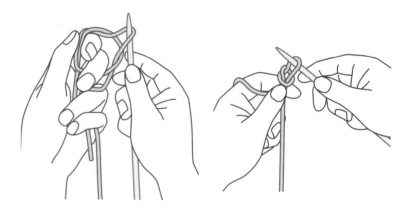

1 First make a slip knot. Wind the yarn around two fingers as shown. Insert a knitting needle over the first strand and under the second strand. Using the needle, pull the strand that is resting on the needle through to the front to form a loop.

2 Holding the loose ends of the yarn with your left hand, pull the needle upwards, to tighten the knot. Pull the ball end of the yarn again to tighten the knot onto the needle.

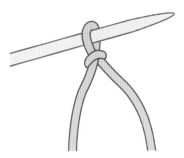

3 The slip knot should be about 15 cm (6 in) from the loose end of the yarn: this is now the first stitch. Hold the needle in your left hand.

4 Insert the point of the right-hand needle from front to back through the slip knot. Pass the yarn from the ball end over the point of the right-hand needle.

5 Bring the point of the right-hand needle with the yarn back through the slip knot, pulling the yarn to make a loop.

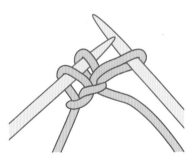

6 Insert the point of the left-hand needle through this loop and remove the right-hand needle, leaving the loop – or second stitch, as it now is – on the left-hand needle. Gently pull the yarn to tighten the stitch.

7 Insert the point of the right-hand needle between the first and second stitches on the left-hand needle. Wind the yarn over the point of the right-hand needle.

8 Pull the loop through and place it on the left-hand needle. Repeat steps 7 and 8 until the required number of stitches has been cast on.

Knit

The knit stitch is the easiest to learn. By knitting every row, you create garter stitch and the simplest of all knitted fabrics.

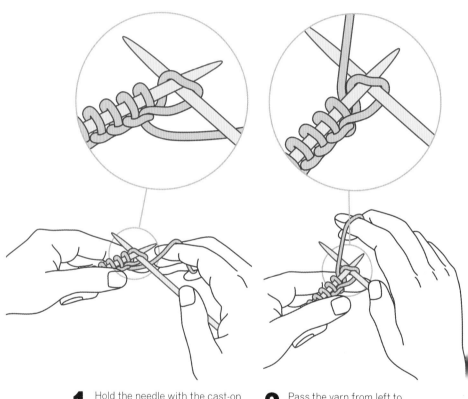

1 Hold the needle with the cast-on stitches in your left hand and the loose yarn at the back of the work. Insert the point of the right-hand needle from left to right through the front of the first stitch on the left-hand needle.

2 Pass the yarn from left to right over the point of the right-hand needle.

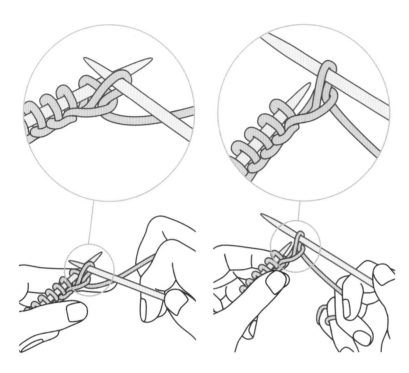

3 Bring the point of the right-hand needle with the yarn back through the stitch, pulling through a loop which makes a new stitch on the right-hand needle.

4 Slip the original stitch off the left-hand needle, keeping the new stitch on the right-hand needle. Pull the yarn end to tighten the stitch onto the needle.

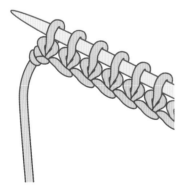

5 Repeat steps 1–4 once into each of the stitches on the left-hand needle, until all the original stitches have been dropped and all the new stitches are on the right-hand needle. You have now knitted your first row.

Turn the needles around so that you are now holding the needle with all the stitches on it in your left hand and the empty needle in your right hand, ready to work the next row in the same way.

Purl

The purl stitch is a little more complicated to master. Using a combination of knit and purl stitches together forms the base of most knitted fabrics. The most common fabric knitted is stocking stitch, created when you knit 1 row, then purl 1 row. Working alternate knit and purl stitch (1 or 2 of each) within a row creates rib, an elastic stitch used in this book for scarves, hat turnback and the wrists of gloves.

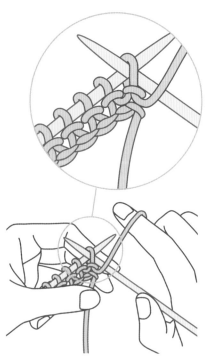

1 Hold the needle with the cast-on stitches in your left hand, with the loose yarn at the front of the work. Insert the point of the right-hand needle from right to left through the front of the first stitch on the left-hand needle.

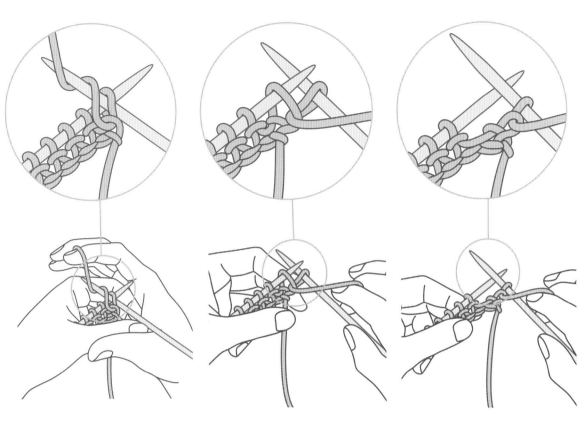

2 Pass the yarn from right to left over the point of the right-hand needle.

3 Bring the point of the right-hand needle with the yarn back through the stitch, pulling through a loop which makes a new stitch on the right-hand needle.

4 Slip the original stitch off the left-hand needle, keeping the new stitch on the right-hand needle. Pull the yarn end to tighten the stitch onto the needle.

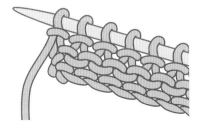

5 Repeat steps 1–4 once into each of the stitches on the left-hand needle, until all the original stitches have been dropped and all the new stitches are on the right-hand needle. You have now purled one row.

Turn the needles around so that you are now holding the needle with all the stitches on it in your left hand and the empty needle in your right hand, ready to work the next row in exactly the same way.

Joining in a new yarn

A new ball of yarn can be joined in on either a right-side or a wrong-side row, but to give a neat finish it is important that you do this at the start of a row. This method is also used for working stripes.

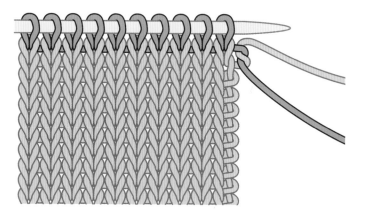

To join in a new yarn, simply drop the old yarn, start knitting with the new ball, and then after a few stitches tie the two ends together in a temporary knot. These ends are then sewn into the knitting at the making-up stage (see page 25).

When using this method for working stripes, when an even number of striped rows is to be knitted don't cut the old yarn – it can be carried up the side of the knitting until you need it again, but make sure you don't pull it too much or you'll distort your knitting.

Decreasing

Decreasing is used in this book mainly to shape the crown on hats. In conjunction with a 'yarn over', it is also used to create eyelets (holes) in lace patterns.

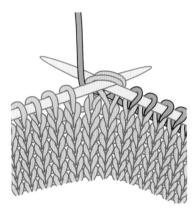

Decreasing on a knit row (K2tog)

Insert the right-hand needle from left to right through two stitches at the same time instead of one, then knit them together as if they were one stitch.

sl1, K1, psso

The other method of decreasing used in this book involves a combination of actions. When you come to this abbreviation, first slip the next stitch onto the right-hand needle (sl1), knit the next stitch (K1), and then pass the slipped stitch over the knitted stitch (psso). This makes one stitch from two, which slants to the left.

Decreasing on a purl row (P2tog)

Insert the right-hand needle from right to left through two stitches at the same time instead of one, then purl them together as if they were one stitch.

yarn over

To make eyelets (holes), decreasing can be used in conjunction with the yarn over (yo) method of increasing, in which the yarn is brought over the needle before working the next stitch, creating an extra loop.

Increasing

This neat method of increasing the number of stitches in a row – called 'make 1' (M1) – is used for shaping, especially in the glove patterns.

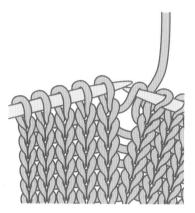 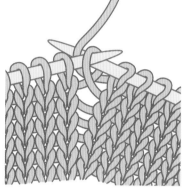

1 With the right-hand needle, lift the strand of yarn that runs between the stitch you've just knitted and the next one on the left-hand needle.

2 Put the strand onto the left-hand needle and then knit it as if it were a normal stitch. This can leave a small hole, so the lifted stitch is usually twisted by working into the back of it, but don't worry if you can't do this.

The procedure is exactly the same on a purl row. With the right-hand needle, lift the strand of yarn that runs between the stitch you've just purled and the next one on the left-hand needle. Put the strand onto the left-hand needle and then purl into the back of it by inserting the point of the right-hand needle from back to front. Slip the original loop off the needle.

Casting off

This is the term used to describe securing the stitches at the top of your knitted fabric. It is important that the cast-off edge is elastic, like the rest of your knitting. If you find that your cast-off is too tight, try using a larger needle. You can cast off knitwise, purlwise, or in a combination of stitches, such as rib – the method described below is for casting off knitwise.

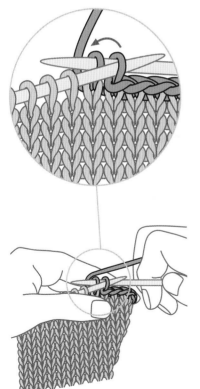

1 Knit the first two stitches as if working a normal knit row. Using the point of the left-hand needle, lift the first stitch over the second stitch and then drop it off the needle. Knit the next stitch and again use the needle point to lift the first stitch over the second stitch. Continue to do this until only one stitch remains on the right-hand needle.

2 Cut the yarn at least 20 cm (8 in) from the stitch, thread the end through the stitch and then slip it off the needle. Draw up the yarn firmly to fasten off.

Finishing techniques

When you have spent many hours knitting, it is essential that you complete your project correctly. Follow the simple instructions provided here to achieve a beautifully finished accessory.

Pressing

It is important to press your knitting before making up, to help maintain the shape of the pieces and achieve a professional-looking finish.

With the wrong side of the fabric facing up, pin out each knitted piece onto an ironing board using the measurements given. If specific measurements are not provided for your project, pin out your knitting neatly without overstretching it and unfurl any edges on scarves that may be rolling up.

As each yarn is different, refer to the ball band and press your knitted pieces according to manufacturer's instructions. Most of the yarns I have used in this book can be pressed. However, if your yarn contains acrylic, it may not be suitable for pressing. Always use a cloth in between the knitting and iron to avoid scorching. Then lightly press or steam the knitted fabric. If you steam your knitting, remember to let it dry completely before removing the pins.

Sewing in ends

Once you have pressed your finished pieces, you will need to sew in all the loose ends. Many knitters find this a very tedious task, but it is well worth putting in the effort. Sew in all ends and don't be tempted to use a long yarn end for sewing up. Always use a separate length of yarn for sewing up. If a mistake is made, you can undo the stitching up without the danger of unravelling all your knitting.

Thread a darning needle with the loose end of yarn, weave the needle along about 5 stitches on the wrong side of the fabric and pull the thread through. Weave the needle in the opposite direction for about 5 stitches, pull the thread through and cut off the end of the yarn neatly.

Making up

Mattress stitch is a method of sewing your knitted pieces together from the right side of the fabric and is ideal for matching stripes accurately.

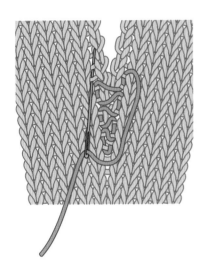

Mattress stitch

For the best finish, mattress stitch should be worked 1 stitch in from the edge of the knitting.

1 With the right side of the knitting facing, lay the pieces to be joined edge to edge. Insert a blunt-tipped needle from the wrong side between the edge stitch and the second stitch. Take the yarn to the opposite piece, insert the needle from the front between the edge stitch and the second stitch, pass the needle under the loops of 2 rows, and bring it back through to the front.

2 Insert the needle under the loops of the corresponding 2 rows in the opposite piece in the same way, and continue this zigzag lacing all along the seam, taking care not to miss any rows.

3 Pull the yarn to close the seam, either after each action or after a few stitches. Take care not to pull it too tight or leave it too loose, as the seam will pucker.

Back stitch

Back stitch is another useful method of making up, this time worked from the wrong side of the knitted fabric.

1 Pin the pieces to be joined with right sides together. Insert a blunt-tipped needle into the knitting at the end, 1 stitch or row from the edge, then take the needle around the two edges to secure them and bring it back up through the fabric. Insert the needle into the fabric just behind where the previous stitch came out and make a short stitch.

2 Re-insert the needle where the previous stitch started and bring it up to make a longer stitch. Re-insert the needle where the previous stitch ended. Repeat to the end, taking care to match any pattern.

Choosing yarns

It is now possible to purchase yarns in two different ways: from yarn shops, or via the Internet (search for 'knitting yarns'). Both offer a huge range of yarns and other products such as needles, buttons, beads and other accessories.

In the knitting patterns in this book, I have specified the yarn I have used, as it is often the particular texture and/or colours that inspired the design. I have used a variety of different yarn types: some for practical reasons, some because of the colour range and some because they are just so luxurious.

Wool is the traditional knitting yarn and comes from the fleece of a sheep. It is very warm to wear and so is great for making hats, gloves and scarves. However, traditionally wool can be quite itchy when you wear it close to the skin, so many yarn spinners now make very soft wool blends using different types of fleece. Look for yarns made from Botany or Merino wool blends, as these are the softest. Some wool yarns are specially treated to make them machine washable, ideal for children's knitting – check the label for washing instructions. If you use a traditional wool yarn that is slightly coarse in texture, it is a good idea to hand wash the finished knitting with some fabric softener: this will make it feel wonderfully soft.

Cotton yarns, made from the cotton plant, are now very popular. The yarn is soft and non-itchy, which is good for children, but it lacks elasticity, so for hats and gloves it does not hold its shape well. Cotton can also be quite heavy so is not practical for very long scarves, but it does feel good against the skin. Some cotton yarn producers also grow 'organic cotton'. This is cotton that is completely natural and has not been treated with dyes. The manufacturers obtain the different shades (soft muted earthy tones, greens and browns) by spinning together similar colour variations.

Wool and cotton mix is a good compromise, offering the softness of cotton combined with the elasticity and heat-retaining properties of wool. It is generally treated to make it machine washable. This yarn is very good for children as it is not itchy.

Wool and cashmere mix feels wonderful to touch and to wear. Cashmere is a luxury fibre and pure cashmere yarns can be expensive, so many spinners combine it with wool to make it more affordable.

Silk is a wonderful fibre and absorbs colour when dyed to produce beautiful vivid shades. However, it is expensive to produce and is often mixed with other yarn fibres.

Mohair comes from the Angora goat and when spun produces a light, fluffy and very warm yarn. Because it is hairy, you can knit this yarn to the same tension as a thicker yarn using bigger needles and the hairy fibres will give the fabric stability.

Angora comes from the Angora rabbit. The luxurious silky hairs are very short and difficult to spin without adding wool or synthetic fibres. As it is expensive to produce, it is rarely used for an entire garment – making it ideal for accessories. Do take care, as the short hairs in this yarn tend to 'shed' and can cause an allergic reaction.

Alpaca is a luxury yarn spun from the fine woolly hairs of llamas found in Bolivia and Peru. It has a soft feel with a slightly hairiness. It most often occurs in knitting yarns as a small percentage added to other fibres for a particular effect.

Synthetic yarns are widely available. Made from man-made fibres, there is a huge range of types and you can find many exciting experimental yarns in wonderful colours. They are great as fun items but are not as long-lasting as natural yarns.

substituting yarns

I have designed the projects in this book using specific yarns as detailed. You may wish to substitute the yarn I have used with one of your own choice. You will need to take care if you do this, as all the patterns are worked out mathematically to the specified yarn. If you substitute a yarn, you must achieve the tension stated in the pattern or your project will turn out too big or too small. Yarns come in various weights such as 4-ply, double knitting and Aran. If substituting a yarn, look for a similar yarn with the same tension – this will be stated on the ball band. It is a good idea to knit a tension square (see page 8) of your chosen yarn before embarking on the design. Having said all this, it can be fun to substitute yarns and start thinking creatively about knitting – especially with the scarves, where you are given a length to work to and no shaping is involved.

Knitting from a chart

The Fairisle hat pattern on page 64 includes both written instructions and a chart. To write out the whole pattern would be very complicated: it is easier to visualize your knitting as the chart and begin to treat it as a picture, 'painting' with coloured yarns.

Reading the chart is easier if you imagine it as the right side of a piece of knitting, working from the lower edge to the top. Each square on the chart represents 1 stitch; each line of squares represents 1 row of knitting. When working from the chart, read odd-numbered rows 1, 3, 5 etc. (right side of fabric) from right to left, and even-numbered rows 2, 4, 6 etc. (wrong side of fabric) from left to right. Each yarn colour used is given a letter in the pattern, which corresponds with a symbol on the chart. This is shown in the key that accompanies the chart.

A ■   B □   C ▦   D ■   E ■   F ■

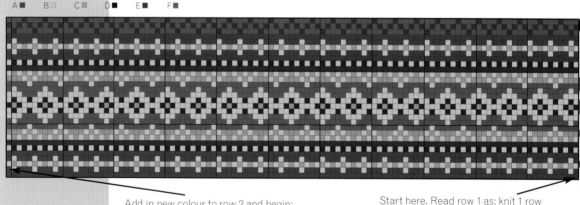

Add in new colour to row 2 and begin: purl 1 stitch using Yarn B, purl 3 stitches using yarn A, continue to work across row.

Start here. Read row 1 as: knit 1 row using Yarn A.

Abbreviations

alt
alternate

beg
begin(ning)

cm
centimetres

cont
continu(e)(ing)

dec
decreas(e)(ing)

foll(s)
follow(s)(ing)

garter st
garter stitch

in
inch(es)

inc
increase(e)(ing)

K2tog
knit 2 stitches together

K
knit

LH
left-hand

M1
make 1 stitch

moss st
moss stitch

P2tog
purl 2 stitches together

P
purl

psso
pass slipped stitch over

rem
remain(ing)

rep
repeat

rev st-st
reversed stocking stitch (purl side of fabric)

RH
right-hand

RS
right side

sl1
slip 1 stitch

st st
stocking stitch

st(s)
stitches

tbl
through back of loop

tog
together

WS
wrong side

yo
yarn over

details

In this book I have aimed to provide as much extra interest as possible by adding a wide range of finishing details to the basic designs and their variations. The techniques used are explained in this chapter.

Pom poms, tassels and cords

Pom poms

1 Decide on the size of pom pom required. Cut two circles of card with a diameter slightly bigger than that of the finished pom pom. Cut a smaller hole in the centre of each circle, about half the size of the original diameter. The larger this hole, the fuller the pom pom will be.

2 Holding the two card rings together, wind the yarn around them (using several strands at a time for speed) until the ring is completely covered. As the hole at the centre gets smaller, you may find it easier to use a darning needle to pass the yarn through.

3 Using a pair of sharp scissors, cut through all the wrapped yarn around the outside edge between the two circles. Make sure all the yarn has been cut.

4 Separate the two circles slightly. Join in a length of knitted cord by wrapping the two tails from one end in opposite directions around the centre of the pom pom and secure firmly with a knot. Pull the two circles apart and fluff out the pom pom to cover the centre join. Trim the pom pom if necessary.

Tassels

1 Cut a rectangle of card as wide as the required length of the finished tassel. Wind the yarn around the card until you reach the required thickness.

2 Break the yarn, thread through a sewing needle and pass the needle under all the loops. Do not remove the needle. Tie the end firmly around the loops, remove the card and cut the loops at the opposite end to the knot.

3 Wind the end of the yarn around all the loops below the fold and fasten securely. Pass the needle through the top of the tassel and use the end to sew it into place. Trim the ends of the tassel neatly.

Fringing

1 Cut lengths of yarn as required, fold the strands in half and draw the folded end through an eyelet (hole) or the centre of a stitch in the hem of the knitting.

2 Draw the loose ends of yarn through the loop, and pull firmly to form a knot.

3 When the fringe is complete, trim the ends.

Knitted cord

1 Using strands of the same colour yarn, cast on 1 stitch. Knit this stitch (K1), turn, K1, turn. This will create a knitted chain (cord) — repeat until you reach the required length of cord.

2 Leave two long tails of yarn at each end of the cord with which to attach pom poms and tassels to your knitting.

Twisted cord

1 Cut three 3 m (10 ft) lengths of yarn and knot the strands together at each end. Attach one end to a hook or door handle and insert a knitting needle through the other end. Twist the needle: the tighter the twisting, the firmer the finished cord will be.

2 Hold the cord in the centre with one hand (you may need some help) and then bring the ends of cord together, allowing the two halves to twist together. Take care to keep the cord straight and avoid tangling. Knot the cut ends together and trim. You can use twisted cord for many things, but attaching it to your gloves or mittens is a sure way of keeping them safe.

Curly cord edging

1 To make this fun edging at the beginning of a piece of knitting, you need to work a curly cord cast on. Using your chosen colour, work as follows: cast on 20 sts, cast off 20 sts, 1 st on LH needle, *cast on 24 sts, cast off 20 sts (5 sts on LH needle), cont to work from * until the desired number of stitches have been cast on.

2 This can be used at the base of a scarf, hat or mittens. If you are knitting a scarf, then you will need to work a curly cord cast off to finish, using your chosen colour: K1, turn and cast on 20 sts, cast off 24 sts knitwise*, work from * to * until all sts are cast off.

Embroidery

Lazy daisy stitch

This embroidery effect is achieved by working individual chain stitches to form petals. These can be grouped together to make a flower of four or five petals, or worked singly to create a leaf. Lazy daisy stitch looks very effective worked either as self-coloured embroidery or in contrast colours.

French knots

Bring the needle from the back to the front of the knitting and wind the yarn several times around the needle, according to the size of knot required. Take the needle back through the same place and draw the yarn through, forming a small knot on the right side of the fabric.

Swiss darning

Swiss darning is a form of embroidery that duplicates the knitted stitches, so that it looks as if the embroidered design has been knitted in.

Working horizontally: Work from left to right. Thread a blunt-tipped needle with embroidery yarn. *Bring the needle out at the base of the first stitch, take it around the top of the stitch under the stitch above, then insert the needle back through the base of the same stitch*, covering the original stitch completely. Repeat this into every stitch along the row.

Working vertically: Work from bottom to top. Work as above from * to *, working into every horizontal stitch to make a vertical line.

There are a multitude of different embroidery techniques that you can apply to your knitting to create different effects. If you are wanting a complicated design, draw it out first on tissue paper and pin this to your piece of knitting. Work the embroidery using different stitches such as cross stitch, stem stitch, chain stitch and satin stitch or a combination of stitches. Use yarns in different colours and textures. Be as creative and inventive as you like. You can add in beads by slipping them onto the yarn in between every stitch which creates a lovely sparkle. To add interest to a plain piece of knitting and finish off the edges, you can also use blanket stitch. Worked in a contrast colour, this is a very effective way of finishing off a design. To keep your embroidery neat, use the stitches and rows of knitting as a guide to size. The key is to be experimental. You can always undo what you have done as embroidery is added after the knitting.

Embellishments

Once you have completed your project, a great way of adding detail is to embellish your knitting – by simply sewing things on. For example, before sewing up the mittens on page 84, I sewed on sequins and beads randomly using silver thread, as well as embroidering star shapes. Using a really basic pattern, such as the Customized hat on page 48, and adding buttons, a spray of feathers and a little butterfly, I have given it a very different look.

By sewing things onto your knitting you can really give your project an individual feel, making it truly unique to you and the wearer. Take time to search through haberdashery shops or the family button box to create a 'treasure chest' of items that you can use. In the future, these could inspire you to create your own inventions.

Knitted flowers

These pretty flowers are created by casting on stitches, and then casting them off on the next row. You can knit them using oddments of yarn, and secure into place by sewing or with a button.

Using yarn and appropriate knitting needles, cast on 36 sts.

Row 1: K1, cast off 4 (2 sts on needle), *K1, cast off 4, rep from * to end. (12 sts on needle)

Thread yarn through rem sts, pull tight and stitch into place.

Lace knitting

The lace patterns in this book are achieved by using the eyelet (yarn over) method of increasing. This is usually worked in conjunction with a decrease, so that the number of stitches remains constant at the end of each row (see page 21). Some patterns in this book are achieved by increasing stitches on some rows and decreasing them on subsequent rows. These are quite complex patterns to work, but the effect is very rewarding.

Ribbon

You can embellish a lace pattern by threading thin ribbon through the eyelets (holes). This is also possible on a standard knitted fabric – simply thread the ribbon through the stitches.

hats

French beret

Frame your face with this elegant beret. Knit it in one colour for classic vintage chic, or add a contemporary twist with stripes in bright colours.

Materials

- **Striped beret**

  One 50 g (2 oz) ball of Rowan 4-ply Soft in each of the following colours: A pink (377 Wink), C berry (374 Honk) and D aqua (373 Splash); and one 25 g (1 oz) ball of Rowan Yorkshire Tweed 4-ply in each of the following colours: B bordeaux (275 Foxy) and E kiwi (272 Butterscotch)

  Pair of 2.75 mm (US 2) knitting needles

  Pair of 3.25 mm (US 3) knitting needles

- **Plain beret**

  Two 25 g (1 oz) balls of Rowan Yorkshire Tweed in blackcurrant (276 Radiant)

  Pair of 2.75 mm (US 2) knitting needles

  Pair of 3.25 mm (US 3) knitting needles

Sizes

- One size (to fit an average adult female head) 56 cm (22 in) circumference

Tension

26 sts x 38 rows to 10 cm (4 in) square measured over using 3.25 mm (US 3) knitting needles

Abbreviations

beg beginning; **foll(s)** follow(s)(ing); **K** knit; **M1** make 1 stitch; **LH** left-hand; **P** purl; **P2tog** purl 2 stitches together; **rem** remain(ing); **rep** repeat; **rev st-st** reversed stocking stitch; **RH** right-hand; **RS** right side; **st(s)** stitch(es); **WS** wrong side

Designer's note

When pressing your beret, cut a disc of card approximately 27 cm (11 in) in diameter, slip it inside the beret and press according to the instructions on the ball band of the yarn used. This will help to maintain the shape of the beret.

The hats

to make

Striped beret

Using 2.75 mm (US 2) knitting needles and yarn A, cast on 146 sts.

Change to yarn B.

Row 1 (RS): K2, [P2, K2] to end.

Row 2: P2, [K2, P2] to end.

Work a further 7 rows in rib as sts set.

Row 10 (WS): Rib 2, [M1, rib 2] to end. 218 sts.

Change to 3.25 mm (US 3) needles. Beg with a purl row, work 20 rows in rev st-st stripe pattern as folls:

2 rows C, 2 rows A, 1 row D, 1 row B, 1 row A, 1 row E, 2 rows B, 1 row E, 1 row A, 1 row B, 1 row D, 2 rows A, 2 rows C, 2 rows B.

Keeping 20-row rev st-st stripe pattern correct throughout, work a further 8 rows. 28 rows rev st-st worked in all.

Shape crown

Next row (RS): [P4, P2tog] to last 2 sts, P2. 182 sts.

Work 13 rows in pattern.

Next row: [P3, P2tog] to last 2 sts, P2. 146 sts.

Work 5 rows in pattern.

Next row: [P2, P2tog] to last 2 sts, P2. 110 sts.

Work 3 rows in pattern.

Next row: [P1, P2tog] to last 2 sts, P2. 74 sts.

Work 3 rows in pattern.

Next row: [P2, P2tog] to last st, P2. 56 sts.

Work 1 row in pattern.

Next row: [P2tog] to last st. 28 sts.

Work 1 row in pattern.

Next row: [P2tog] to end. 14 sts.

Break off yarn, run yarn through rem sts, draw up and fasten off.

To match stripes neatly, sew up seam using mattress stitch.

Plain beret

Using 2.75 mm (US 2) knitting needles, work picot cast-on as folls:

Cast on 5 sts, cast off 2 sts, slip st on RH needle back onto LH needle (3 sts now on LH needle), rep from * to * until 144 sts on needle, cast on 2 sts. 146 sts

Now complete as for Striped beret, working in one colour only.

Winter warmer

Out for a walk on a snowy day, your outfit is not complete without a traditional ribbed hat. Add some fabulous pom poms and let the snowballs fly.

Materials

- **Blue hat**

    Two 50 g (2 oz) balls of Jaeger Matchmaker Merino Aran in sky (770 Ice)

    Pair of 4.5 mm (US 7) knitting needles

    Two 4.5 cm (1¾ in) and five 3.5 cm (1¼ in) pom poms made using one 50 g (2 oz) ball of Jaeger Matchmaker Merino Aran in navy (629 Mariner)

- **Camel hat**

    Two 50 g (2 oz) balls of Jaeger Matchmaker Merino Aran in camel (766 Soft Camel)

    Pair of 4.5 mm (US 7) knitting needles

    6.5 cm (2½ in) pom pom

Sizes

- Small (to fit child aged 5 upwards)

    46 cm (18 in) circumference

- Medium (to fit average adult female head)

    56 cm (22 in) circumference

Tension

24 sts x 26 rows to 10 cm (4 in) square measured over rib pattern using 4.5 mm (US 7) knitting needles

Abbreviations

dec decreas(e)(ing); **K** knit; **k2tog** knit 2 stitches together; **P** purl; **P2tog** purl 2 sts together; **RS** right side; **st(s)** stitch(es); **WS** wrong side

Designer's note

To use up oddments of yarn, this hat would also look really cute knitted in different-coloured stripes. The pom poms could then be worked in a range of sizes and colours.

Working instructions

Pattern is written for small size first with medium size in brackets.

The hats

to make

Using 4.5 mm (US 7) knitting needles, cast on 80(92) sts.

Rib row 1 (RS): K1, [K4, P2] 13(15) times, K1.

Rib row 2: K1, [K2, P4] 12(15) times, K1.

These 2 rows set the rib sts. Work these 2 rows until work measures 18(21) cm (7(8¼) in) from cast-on, ending with a WS row.

Shape crown

Next row (dec): K1, [K4, P2tog] 13(15) times, K1. 67(77) sts.

Work 3 rows as sts set.

Next row (dec): K1, [K1, K2tog, K1, P1] 13(15) times, K1. 54(62) sts.

Work 1 row.

Next row (dec): K1, [K1, K2tog, P1] 13(15) times, K1. 41(47) sts.

Work 1 row.

Next row (dec): K1, [K2tog, P1] 13(15) times, K1. 28(32) sts.

Work 1 row.

Next row (dec): K1, [K2tog] 13(15) times, K1. 15(17) sts.

Work 1 row.

Next row (dec): [K2tog] to last st, K1. 8(9) sts.

Break off yarn, run yarn through rem sts, draw up and fasten off. Using knit stitch selvedge as a guide, sew seam using mattress stitch (or back stitch if preferred), reversing seam for bottom 5 cm (2 in) for hat turn–back.

to finish

Make the pom poms as described on page 32. Using the photograph as a guide, decorate the hat with pom poms. For the blue hat, make 7 knitted or crochet cords (see page 33). Attach one end of one cord to a pom pom and the other end of the cord to the top of the hat.

Sitting pretty

Glamorous, simple and stylish are the words that define these three hats. Knit the one that best suits your style – whichever it is, you'll be sitting pretty.

Materials

- **Lace-edged hat**

  Two 50 g (2 oz) balls of Debbie Bliss Cashmere Aran in rose (602)

  Pair of 4.5 mm (US 7) knitting needles

- **Embroidered hat**

  Two 50 g (2 oz) balls of Debbie Bliss Cashmere Aran in cherry (611)

  Pair of 4.5 mm (US 7) knitting needles

  Large-eyed darning needle

- **Customized hat**

  Two 50 g (2 oz) balls of Debbie Bliss Cashmere Aran in ice (202)

  Pair of 4.5 mm (US 7) knitting needles

  1 m (1¼ yd) velvet ribbon, 7.5 mm (¼ in) wide

  11 small mother-of-pearl buttons

  Selection of feathers

  Small velvet butterfly

  Sewing needle and thread

Sizes

- One size (to fit average adult female head)

  56 cm (22 in) circumference

Tension

20 sts x 26 rows to 10 cm (4 in) square measured over st-st using 4.5 mm (US 7) knitting needles

Abbreviations

alt alternate; **cont** continu(e)(ing); **dec** decreas(e)(ing); **foll** follow(s)(ing); **K** knit; **K2tog** knit 2 stitches together; **LH** left-hand **P** purl; **rem** remain(ing); **psso** pass slipped stitch over; **rep** repeat; **RH** right-hand; **RS** right side; **sl1** slip 1 stitch; **st(s)** stitch(es); **st-st** stocking stitch; **WS** wrong side; **yo** yarn over

Designer's note

The basic pattern of this hat is very simple – here I have given it three very different looks. Why not experiment with your own edging ideas? I have used pearl buttons and ribbon from my grandma's button box for the Customized hat, but see what materials you can find to make your own hat unique.

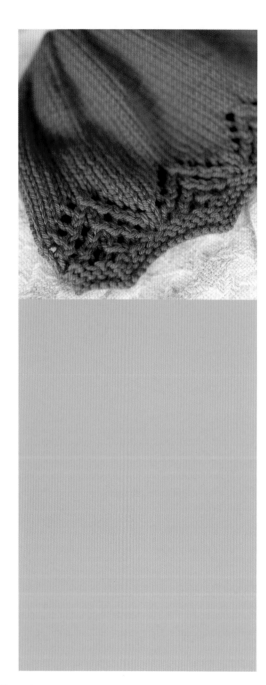

The hats

to make

Lace-edged hat

Using 4.5 mm (US 7) knitting needles, cast on 128 sts.

Row 1 (RS) (dec): K1, (sl1, K1, psso, K9, K2tog, K1) 9 times, K1. (110 sts)

Row 2: Knit.

Row 3 (dec): K1, (sl1, K1, psso, K7, K2tog, K1) 9 times, K1. (92 sts)

Row 4: Knit.

Row 5: K1, ([yo, sl1, K1, psso] twice, K1, [K2tog, yo] twice, K1) 9 times, K1.

Row 6 and every WS row: K1, P to last st, K1

Row 7: K1, (K1, yo, sl1, K1, psso , yo, sl1, K2tog, psso, yo, K2tog, yo, K2) 9 times, K1.

Row 9: K1, ([yo, sl1, K1, psso] twice, K1, [K2tog, yo] twice, K1) 9 times, K1.

Row 11: K1, (K1, yo, sl1, K1, psso , yo, sl1, K2tog, psso, yo, K2tog, yo, K2) 9 times, K1.

Row 13: K1, (K2, yo, sl1, K1, psso, K1, K2tog, yo, K3) 9 times, K1.

Row 15: K1, (K3, yo, sl1, K2tog, psso, yo, K4) 9 times, K1.

Row 16: K1, P to last st, K1.

Row 17: Knit.

Row 18: K1, P to last st, K1.

Rep last 2 rows until hat measures 13 cm (5 in), ending with a WS row. See page 52 for shaping crown instructions.

Embroidered hat

Using 4.5 mm (US 7) knitting needles, work picot cast-on as folls: *Cast on 5 sts, cast off 2 sts, slip st on RH needle back onto LH needle* [3 sts now on LH needle], rep from * to * until 90 sts on needle, cast on 2 sts. 92 sts.

Rows 1–4: Knit.

Row 5: Knit.

Row 6: K1, P to last st, K1.

Rep last 2 rows until hat measures 13 cm (5 in), ending with a WS row. See page 52 for shaping crown instructions.

Customized hat

Using 4.5 mm (US 7) knitting needles, cast on 92 sts.

Row 1 (RS): Knit.

Row 2: Knit.

Row 3: Knit.

Row 4: K1, P1, (P2, yo, P2tog) 22 times, P1, K1.

Row 5: Knit.

Row 6: Knit.

Row 7: Knit.

Row 8: K1, P to last st, K1.

Rep last 2 rows until hat measures 13 cm (5 in), ending with a WS row.

See below for shaping crown instructions.

All hats

Shape crown

Row 1 (RS): K1, [K7, K2tog] 10 times, K1. 82 sts.

Row 2 and every alt row: K1, P to last st, K1.

Row 3: K1, [K6, K2tog] 10 times, K1. 72 sts.

Row 5: K1, [K5, K2tog] 10 times, K1. 62 sts.

Cont to dec as above on every alt row until 12 sts rem.

Break off yarn, run yarn through rem sts, draw up and fasten off.

Using knit stitch selvedge as a guide, sew seam using mattress stitch (or back stitch).

to finish

Embroidered hat

Using a large-eyed darning needle, work self-coloured lazy daisy and French knot embroidery around the edge of the hat.

Customized hat

Thread ribbon through the eyelets (holes) and secure with a bow on the left–hand side. Sew on buttons between the eyelets. Decorate with feathers and a butterfly as shown in the photograph, securing in place with small stitches on the reverse of the hat.

Streamlined sporty

On your marks, get set... go! Start those needles clicking and create the perfect hat for an afternoon jog in the park – or perhaps just a leisurely stroll.

Materials

- **Plain hat**

  Two 50 g (2 oz) balls of Jaeger Extra Fine Merino in brown fleck (974 Tabby)

  Pair of 3.25 mm (US 3) knitting needles

  Pair of 4 mm (US 6) knitting needles

- **Lady's narrow-striped hat**

  One 50 g (2 oz) ball of Jaeger Extra Fine Merino in each of the following colours: A pink (982 Rose Petal), B beige (973 Biscuit) and C blue (940 Ocean)

  Pair of 3.25 mm (US 3) knitting needles

  Pair of 4 mm (US 6) knitting needles

- **Man's wide-striped hat**

  One 50 g (2 oz) ball of Jaeger Extra Fine Merino in each of the following colours: A burgundy (944 Elderberry) and B blue (945 Blackcurrant)

  Pair of 3.25 mm (US 3) knitting needles

  Pair of 4 mm (US 6) knitting needles

Sizes

- Medium (to fit an average adult female head) 56 cm (22 in) circumference
- Large (to fit an average adult male head) 61 cm (24 in) circumference

Tension

22 sts x 30 rows to 10 cm (4 in) square measured over st-st using 4 mm (US 6) knitting needles

Abbreviations

alt alternate; **cont** continu(e)(ing); **dec** decreas(e)(ing); **foll** follow(s)(ing); **inc** increas(e)(ing); **K** knit; **K2tog** knit 2 stitches together; **P** purl; **rem** remain(ing); **rep** repeat; **RS** right side; **st(s)** stitch(es); **st-st** stocking stitch; **tbl** through back of loops; **WS** wrong side

Designer's note

This hat pattern is extremely simple: try knitting it for a soccer fan using the team colours in the stripes, or as a gift in one colour to co-ordinate with the recipient's favourite sweater, coat, handbag or shoes.

Working instructions

Pattern is written for medium size (narrow stripe) first with large size (wide stripe) in brackets. Work the Plain hat in the appropriate size but in one colour throughout.

The hats
to make

Using 3.25 mm (US 3) knitting needles and yarn C(A), cast on 114(126) sts. Change to (keep) yarn A and work rib as folls:

Row 1 (RS): K3, P3 to end.

Row 2: K3, P3 to end.

These 2 rows set the rib sts. Work these 2 rows 4 times more.

Change to 4 mm (US 6) knitting needles. Starting with a K row, work in st-st following chosen stripe pattern:

Narrow stripe

2 rows B, 2 rows C, 2 rows A.

Wide stripe

12 rows B, 12 rows A.

Cont until work measures 10 cm (4 in) from cast-on.

Keeping stripe sequence correct, work shaping for crown.

Shape crown

Next row: K7(8), [K2tog tbl, K1, K2tog, K14(16)] 5 times, K2tog tbl, K1, K2tog, K7(8). 102(114) sts.

Work 3 rows.

Next row: K6(7), [K2tog tbl, K1, K2tog, K12(14)] 5 times, K2tog tbl, K1, K2tog, K6(7).

90(102) sts.

Work 3 rows.

Next row: K5(6), [K2tog tbl, K1, K2tog, K10(12)] 5 times, K2tog tbl, K1, K2tog, K5(6). 78(90) sts.

Work 3 rows.

Next row: K4(5), [K2tog tbl, K1, K2tog, K8(10)] 5 times, K2tog tbl, K1, K2tog, K4(5). 66(78) sts.

Work 1(3) row(s).

Next row: K3(4), [K2tog tbl, K1, K2tog, K6(8)] 5 times, K2tog tbl, K1, K2tog, K3(4). 54(66) sts.

Work 1 row.

Cont to dec as above on every alt row until 18 sts rem, ending with a RS row.

Next row (WS): [P3tog] 6 times. 6 sts. Break off yarn, run yarn through rem sts, draw up and fasten off.

Using the knit stitch selvedge as a guide, sew seam using mattress stitch (or back stitch if preferred).

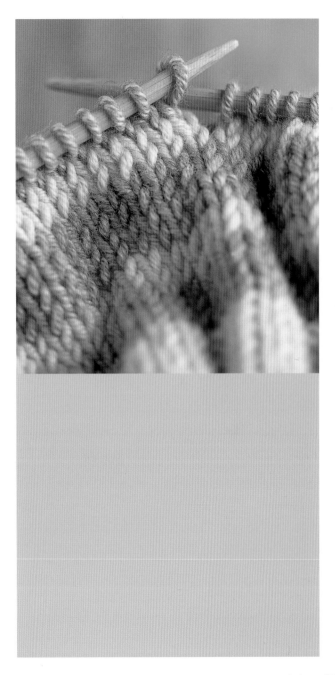

Cute in cable

Pull on this cute cabled hat, look out from under the generous brim and watch all the attention turn to you – not the dog you're walking.

Materials

- **Orange hat**

  One 50 g (2 oz) ball of Rowan Kid Classic in orange (827 Juicy)

  Pair of 5 mm (US 8) knitting needles

  Tassel

- **Purple hat**

  One 50 g (2 oz) ball of Rowan Kid Classic in purple (835 Royal)

  Pair of 5 mm (US 8) knitting needles

  Tassel

Sizes

- One size (to fit child aged 9 years, up to an average adult female head)

  51–56 cm (20–22 in) circumference

Tension

17 sts x 24 rows to 10 cm (4 in) square measured over st-st using 5 mm (US 8) knitting needles

Abbreviations

alt alternate; **dec** decreas(e)(ing); **foll(s)** follow(s)(ing); **inc** increas(e)(ing); **K** knit; **M1** make 1 st; **P** purl; **P2tog** purl 2 sts together; **psso** pass slipped stitch over; **rem** remain(ing); **rep** repeat; **RS** right side; **sl1** slip 1 stitch; **st(s)** stitch(es); **st-st** stocking stitch; **WS** wrong side

Special abbreviation: C6F cable 6 forward – slip 3 sts onto cable needle, hold at front, K3, then K3 from cable needle

Designer's note

To change the look of this hat you could knit the rib in a contrast colour. If you are feeling really confident, you could also try knitting the cables in a different colour – this would require a little more skill and knitting in vertical stripes using separate balls of yarn for each colour.

The hats

to make

Using 5 mm (US 8) knitting needles, cast on 82 sts.

Rib row 1 (RS): K1, [K4, P4] 10 times, K1.

Rib row 2: K1, [K4, P4] 10 times, K1.

These 2 rows set the rib sts. Work these 2 rows until work measures 6 cm (2¼ in) from cast-on, ending with a WS row.

Now work cable pattern as folls:

Row 1: K1, [P12, K4] 5 times, K1.

Row 2: K1, [P4, K12] 5 times, K1.

Row 3 (inc): K1, [P12, K1, M1, K2, M1, K1] 5 times, K1. 92 sts.

Row 4 and every foll alt row: K1, [P6, K12] 5 times, K1.

Row 5: K1, [P12, K6] 5 times, K1.

Row 7: K1, [P12, C6F] 5 times, K1.

Row 9: K1, [P12, K6] 5 times, K1.

Row 11: K1, [P12, K6] 5 times, K1.

Row 13: K1, [P12, K6] 5 times, K1.

Row 14: K1, [P6, K12] 5 times, K1.

Rep rows 7–14 twice more.

Shape crown

Next row (RS) (dec): K1, [P2 tog, P8, P2tog, C6F] 5 times, K1. 82 sts.

Next row: K1, [P6, K10] 5 times, K1.

Next row (dec): K1, [P2 tog, P6, P2tog, K6] 5 times, K1. 72 sts.

Next row: K1, [P6, K8] 5 times, K1.

Next row (dec): K1, [P2 tog, P4, P2tog, K6] 5 times, K1. 62 sts.

Next row: K1, [P6, K6] 5 times, K1.

Next row (dec): K1, [P2 tog, P2, P2tog, K6] 5 times, K1. 52 sts.

Next row: K1, [P6, K4] 5 times, K1.

Next row (dec): K1, [P2 tog, P2tog, C6F] 5 times, K1. 42 sts.

Next row: K1, [P6, K2] 5 times, K1.

Next row (dec): K1, [P2, K1, sl1, K1, psso, K2tog, K1] 5 times, K1. 32 sts.

Next row: K1, [P4, K2] 5 times, K1.

Next row (dec): K1, [P2, sl1, K1, psso, K2tog] 5 times, K1. 22 sts.

Next row: K1, [P2, K2] 5 times, K1.

Next row (dec): K1, [K2tog] 10 times, K1. 12 sts.

Next row: K1, purl to last st, K1.

Break off yarn, run yarn through rem sts, draw up and fasten off.

Using knit stitch selvedge as a guide, sew seam using mattress stitch (or back stitch if preferred), reversing seam for bottom 6 cm (2¼ in) for hat turn-back.

to finish

Make the tassel as described on page 32. Using the photograph as a guide, attach the tassel to the top of the hat.

Fancy Fairisle

Whether promenading city streets or returning from the slopes for *après-ski*, this hat will keep your head warm while you look extremely cool.

Materials

- **Blue hat**

  One 50 g (2 oz) ball of Jaeger Matchmaker DK in each of the following colours: A blue (889 Pacific), B aqua (865 Sea Foam), C red (656 Cherry), D navy (2346 Mid Navy), E lime (899 Hop) and F mid-blue (629 Mariner)
  Pair of 3.25 mm (US 3) knitting needles
  Pair of 4.5 mm (US 7) knitting needles
  4.5 cm (1³/₄ in) pom pom

- **Red hat**

  One 50 g (2 oz) ball of Jaeger Matchmaker DK in each of the following colours: A brick (876 Clarice), B camel (865 Soft Camel), C orange (901 Rusty), D brown (728 Bison), E burgundy (655 Burgundy) and F red (656 Cherry)
  Pair of 3.25 mm (US 3) knitting needles
  Pair of 4.5 mm (US 7) knitting needles

Sizes

- One size (to fit child aged 9 years, up to an average adult female head) 51–56 cm (20–22 in) circumference

Tension

24 sts x 26 rows to 10 cm (4 in) square measured over Fairisle patt using 4.5 mm (US 7) knitting needles

Abbreviations

dec decreas(e)(ing); **garter st** garter stitch; **K** knit; **K2tog** knit 2 stitches together; **P** purl; **rem** remain(ing); **RS** right side; **st(s)** stitch(es); **WS** wrong side

Designer's note

This hat pattern is knitted using the Fairisle technique, which gives it a very Alpine look. It is important to follow these tips when you are knitting Fairisle:

- When knitting two colours across a row, strand the yarn not in use loosely behind the stitches being worked.
- Spread your stitches as you are knitting to keep the fabric elastic. This technique takes a little more effort, but looks beautiful when finished.

The hats

to make

Using 3.25 mm (US 3) knitting needles and yarn F, cast on 111 sts.

Change to yarn E and work in garter st, setting sts as folls:

Row 1 (RS): Knit.

Row 2: Knit.

Work 4 more rows in garter st.

Change to 4.5 mm (US 7) knitting needles and work 30 rows in Fairisle pattern from chart, joining in and breaking off colours as required.

Shape crown

Row 1 (RS) (dec): [K9, K2tog] 10 times, K1 using Yarn A. 101 sts.

Row 2: Purl using Yarn A.

Row 3: [K8, K2tog] 10 times, K1 using Yarn E. 91 sts.

Row 4: [P1 using yarn D, P1 using yarn B] to end.

Row 5: [K7, K2tog] 10 times, K1 using Yarn C. 81 sts.

Row 6: Purl using Yarn C.

Row 7: [K6, K2tog] 10 times, K1 using Yarn F. 71 sts.

Row 8: Purl using Yarn F.

Row 9: [K5, K2tog] 10 times, K1 using Yarn A. 61 sts.

Row 10: Purl using Yarn A.

Row 11: [K4, K2tog]) 10 times, K1, using Yarn B. 51 sts.

Row 12: [P1 using yarn D, P1 using yarn C] to end.

Row 13: [K3, K2tog] 10 times, K1 using Yarn A. 41 sts.

Row 14: Purl using Yarn A.

Row 15: [K2, K2tog] 10 times, K1 using Yarn F. 31 sts.

Row 16: Purl using Yarn F.

Row 17: [K1, K2tog] 10 times, K1 using Yarn C. 21 sts.

Row 18: Purl using Yarn C.

Row 19: [K2tog] 10 times, K1 using Yarn E. 11 sts.

Row 20: Purl using Yarn E.

Break off yarn, run yarn through rem sts, draw up
and fasten off.

Sew seam using mattress stitch on RS to match
Fairisle pattern neatly (or back stitch if preferred).

to finish

Blue hat

Make a 4.5 cm (2 in) pom pom as described on page
32, using your choice of colour. Using the photograph
as a guide, attach the pom pom to the top of the hat.

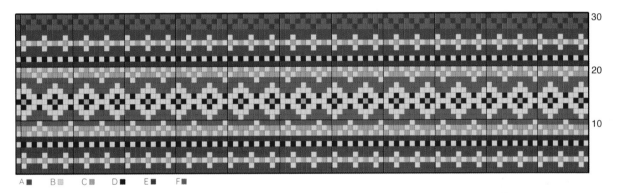

Work odd numbered rows as knit rows, reading the chart from right to left.

Work even numbered rows as purl rows, reading the chart from left to right.

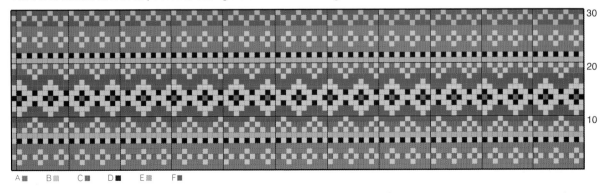

Beanie for all

You can knit this hat for all the family, customizing it to suit the individual or creating a matching set in one favourite colour.

Materials

- **Striped hat**

  One 50 g (2 oz) ball of Rowan Wool Cotton in each of the following colours: A navy (909 French Navy), B aqua (949 Aqua), C green (955 Ship Shape)

  Pair of 3.25 mm (US 3) knitting needles

  Pair of 4 mm (US 6) knitting needles

- **Plain hat**

  Two 50 g (2 oz) balls of Rowan Wool Cotton in grey marl (903 Misty)

  Pair of 3.25 mm (US 3) knitting needles

  Pair of 4 mm (US 6) knitting needles

- **Plain hat with flower corsage**

  Two 50 g (2 oz) balls of Rowan Wool Cotton in lavender (954 Grand)

  Pair of 3.25 mm (US 3) knitting needles

  Pair of 4 mm (US 6) knitting needles

  Two flowers, knitted using Rowan Wool Cotton in lilac (952 Hiss)

  Brooch back

  25 clear glass beads

- **Plain hat with lazy daisy embroidery**

  Two 50 g (2 oz) balls of Rowan Wool Cotton in raspberry (959 Bilberry Fool)

  Pair of 3.25 mm (US 3) knitting needles

  Pair of 4 mm (US 6) knitting needles

  Small amount of pink yarn, for lazy daisy embroidery

  Large-eyed darning needle

Sizes

- Extra-small 46 cm (18 in) circumference
- Small 51 cm (20 in) circumference
- Medium 56 cm (22 in) circumference
- Large 61 cm (24 in) circumference

Tension

22 sts x 30 rows to 10 cm (4 in) square measured over st-st using 4 mm (US 6) knitting needles

Abbreviations

alt alternate; **cont** continu(e)(ing); **dec** decreas(e)(ing); **foll(s)** follow(s)(ing); **K** knit; **K2tog** knit 2 stitches together; **P** purl; **rem** remaining; **RS** right side; **st(s)** stitch(es); **st-st** stocking stitch; **WS** wrong side

Working instructions

The pattern is written for the Striped hat in four sizes: extra-small first, followed by small, medium and large in brackets. Work the Plain hats in the appropriate size but in one colour throughout.

The hats

to make

Striped hat

Using 3.25 mm (US 3) knitting needles and yarn A, cast on 92(102,112,122) sts.

Row 1 (RS): Knit.

Row 2: K1, P to last st, K1.

These 2 rows set the pattern. Work 6 more rows ending with WS row.

Change to 4 mm (US 6) knitting needles, and work stripe pattern as folls:

4 rows B, 4 rows C, 4 rows A.

Keeping stripe sequence correct, cont in pattern until work measures 10(12,14,16) cm (4(4¾,5½,6¼) in), ending with a WS row.

Shape crown

Row 1 (RS) (dec): K1, [K7(8,9,10), K2tog] 10 times, K1. 82(92,102,112) sts.

Row 2 and every alt row: K1, P to last st, K1.

Row 3 (RS) (dec): K1, [K6(7,8,9) K2tog] 10 times, K1. 72(82,92,102) sts.

Row 4 (RS) (dec): K1, [K5(6,7,8), K2tog] 10 times, K1. 62(72,82,92) sts.

Cont to dec as above on every alt row until 12 sts rem. Break off yarn, run yarn through rem sts, draw up and fasten off.

Using yarn thread through stitches, make a knitted cord approximately 4 cm (1½ in) long. Form into a small loop in centre of hat and sew in place before stitching up (optional).

Using knit stitch selvedge as a guide, sew seam using mattress stitch (or back stitch if preferred), reversing seam for bottom 4 cm (1½ in) for hat roll-back.

to finish

Plain hat with flower corsage

Using 4 mm (US 6) knitting needles, make two flowers as described on page 36. Sew the flowers together and attach to the brooch back. Decorate the flower centres using the clear glass beads. Pin the corsage onto the hat.

Plain hat with lazy daisy embroidery

Using a large-eyed darning needle and contrast yarn shade, work lazy daisy embroidery around the hat as shown in the photograph.

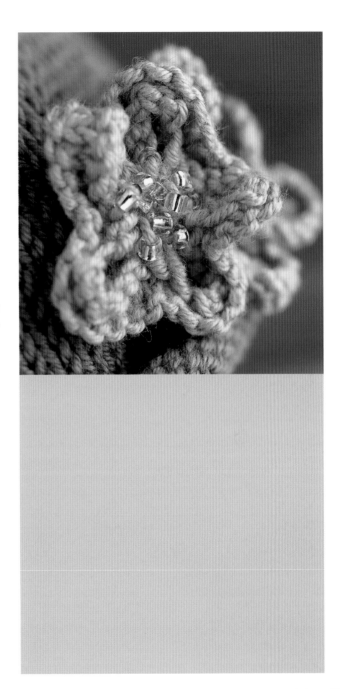

Brimming with style

One simple pattern and one very chic yarn complete this stylish yet understated hat – but you will certainly not go unnoticed.

Materials

One 100 g (4 oz) ball of Rowan Chunky Print in brown (080 Pit)

Pair of 6 mm (US 10) knitting needles

Sizes

• One size (to fit an average adult female head) 56 cm (22 in) circumference

Tension

14 sts x 24 rows to 10 cm (4 in) square measured over moss st using 6 mm (US 10) knitting needles

Abbreviations

alt alternate; **cont** continu(e)(ing); **dec** decreas(e)(ing); **K** knit; **K2tog** knit 2 stitches together; **moss st** moss stitch; **LH** left-hand; **P** purl; **rem** remain(ing); **rep** repeat; **RS** right side; **st(s)** stitch(es); **WS** wrong side

Special abbreviation: wrap st wrap next stitch – slip next st, take yarn to opposite side of work between needles, slip same st back onto LH needle; when working back across wrapped st, work loop and st made together as one st, turn.

Designer's note

This pattern is very contemporary and would be great knitted in a bright marled print yarn, or you could combine lots of finer-weight yarns together to make a really thick one. The fabric is knitted in a firm moss stitch, so the hat will maintain its shape during wearing but is flexible enough to fold up and pack in a handbag.

The hat

to make

Brim (worked sideways)

Using 6 mm (US 10) knitting needles, cast on 21 sts.

Row 1 (RS): [K1, P1] 10 times, K1.

Row 2: [K1, P1] 5 times, K3, [P1, K1] 4 times.

Row 3: [K1, P1] 4 times, wrap st, turn.

Row 4: [P1, K1] 4 times.

Row 5: [K1, P1] 10 times, K1.

Row 6: [K1, P1] 5 times, K3, [P1, K1] 4 times.

The last 6 rows form the moss st pattern.

Rep these 6 rows until work measures 46 cm (18 in) on shorter edge from cast-on, ending with a WS row. Cast off in moss st.

Shape crown

With WS facing and using 6 mm (US 10) needles, and working 1 st in along shorter side length of brim, pick up and knit 72 sts.

Next row (RS): Knit.

Next row: K1, P to last st, K1.

Next row (RS) (dec): K1, [K5, K2tog] 10 times, K1. 62 sts.

Next row and every alt row: K1, P to last st, K1.

Next row: K1, [K4, K2tog] 10 times, K1. 52 sts.

Cont to dec as above on every alt row until 12 sts rem.

Next row: K1, P to last st, K1.

Next row: [K2tog] to end. 6 sts.

Break off yarn, run yarn through rem sts, draw up and fasten off.

Using knit stitch selvedge on crown as a guide, sew seam using back stitch.

gloves

Frivolous fingers

Tap them, wiggle them, wave them: you can let your fingers do the talking in these fun and elegant fingerless gloves.

Materials

• Standard gloves

One 25 g (1 oz) ball of Rowan Kid Silk Haze in colour A soft purple (600 Dewberry)* and one 50 g (2 oz) ball of RYC Cashmino DK in colour B grey (518 Thunder)

*This yarn is used double throughout

Pair of 4 mm (US 6) knitting needles

• Extra-long gloves

One 25 g (1 oz) ball of Rowan Kid Silk Haze in colour A soft green (581 Meadow)* and one 50 g (2 oz) ball of RYC Cashmino DK in colour B khaki (516 Sage)

*This yarn is used double throughout

Pair of 4 mm (US 6) knitting needles

0.5 m (½yd) velvet ribbon, 7.5 mm (¼in) wide

Sizes

• One size (to fit an average adult female hand)

Tension

22 sts x 30 rows to 10 cm (4 in) square measured over st-st using 4 mm (US 6) knitting needles

Abbreviations

cont continu(e)(ing); **dec** decreas(e)(ing); **foll(s)** follow(s)(ing); **inc** increas(e)(ing); **K** knit; **K2tog** knit 2 stitches together; **LH** left-hand; **M1** make 1 stitch; **P** purl; **rem** remain(ing); **rep** repeat; **RH** right-hand; **RS** right side; **st(s)** stitch(es); **st-st** stocking stitch; **tbl** through back of loop; **WS** wrong side

Designer's note

These gloves are knitted in gorgeous yarns – silk and mohair, and a cashmere mix – and when knitted together in the stripe combination they feel really luxurious. I have threaded a ribbon through the long gloves for a 'retro' feel. Alternatively, the gloves could be knitted in one colour throughout using two balls of the RYC Cashmino DK yarn.

The gloves

to make

Standard gloves right glove

Using 4 mm (US 6) knitting needles and yarn A, work picot cast-on as folls:

Cast on 5 sts, cast off 2 sts, slip st on RH needle back onto LH needle (3 sts now on LH needle), rep from * to * until 36 sts on needle, cast on 1 st. 37 sts.

Using yarn A:

Row 1: Knit.

Row 2: K1, P to last st, K1.

These 2 rows set the pattern.

Now work in stripe pattern as folls:

2 rows A, 2 rows B.

Keeping stripe sequence correct, cont in pattern until 20 stripe rows (22 rows from cast on) have been worked, ending with a WS row.**

Standard gloves left glove

Work as for Standard gloves right glove to **.

Extra-long gloves right glove

Using 4 mm (US 6) knitting needles and yarn A, cast on 41 sts.

Using yarn A:

Row 1: Knit.

Row 2: K1, P to last st, K1.

These 2 rows set the pattern. Now work in stripe pattern as folls:

2 rows A, 2 rows B.

Keeping stripe sequence correct, cont in pattern until 20 stripe rows (22 rows from cast-on) have been worked, ending with a WS row.

Next row (RS) (dec): K3, K2tog, knit to last 5 sts, K2tog tbl, K3. 39 sts.

Work 19 more rows in stripe pattern.

Next row (RS) (dec): K3, K2tog, knit to last 5 sts, K2tog tbl, K3. 37 sts.

Work 19 more rows in stripe pattern.**

Extra-long gloves left glove

Work as for Extra-long gloves right glove to **.

Both right gloves

Shape thumb

Row 1 (RS): K19, M1, K3, M1, K15. 39 sts.

Work 3 rows in stripe pattern.

Row 5 (RS): K19, M1, K5, M1, K15. 41 sts.

Work 3 rows in stripe pattern.

Cont to inc as above on next row and every foll 4th row to 47 sts.

Next row: Purl.

Knit thumb

Next row (RS): K32, turn.

Next row: P13.

Working on these 13 sts only, work 9 rows in stripe pattern.

Cast off knitwise. Join thumb seam.

With RS facing, rejoin yarn, pick up and knit 2 sts from base of thumb and K to end. 36 sts.

Next row: Purl.

Work 8 rows in stripe pattern.

Knit first finger

Next row (RS): K23, turn, cast on 1 st.

Next row: P11, turn cast on 1 st. 12 sts.

Working on these 12 sts only, work 9 rows in stripe pattern.

Cast off knitwise. Join finger seam.

Knit second finger

With RS facing, rejoin yarn, pick up and knit 2 sts from base of finger, K4 sts, turn, cast on 1 st.

Next row: P11, turn, cast on 1 st. 12 sts.

Working on these 12 sts only, work 9 rows in stripe pattern.

Cast off knitwise. Join finger seam.

Knit third finger

With RS facing, rejoin yarn, pick up and knit 2 sts from base of finger, K4 sts, turn, cast on 1 st.

Next row: P11, turn cast on 1 st. 12 sts.

Working on these 12 sts only, work 9 rows in stripe pattern.

Cast off knitwise. Join finger seam.

Knit fourth finger

With RS facing, rejoin yarn to rem sts, pick up and knit 2 sts from base of finger, K to end.

Next row: K1, P10, K1. 12 sts.

Working on these 12 sts only, work 7 rows in stripe pattern.

Cast off knitwise.

Using knit stitch selvedge as a guide, sew finger and side seams using mattress stitch on RS to match stripes neatly (or back stitch if preferred).

Both left gloves

Shape thumb

Row 1 (RS): K15, M1, K3, M1, K19. 39 sts.

Work 3 rows in stripe pattern.

Row 5 (RS): K15, M1, K5, M1, K19. 41 sts.

Work 3 rows in stripe pattern.

Cont to inc as above on next row and every foll 4th row to 47 sts.

Next row: Purl.

Divide for thumb

Next row (RS): K28, turn.

Next row: P13.

Working on these 13 sts only, work 9 rows in stripe pattern.

Cast off knitwise. Join thumb seam.

With RS facing, rejoin yarn, pick up and knit 2 sts from base of thumb and K to end. 36 sts.

Next row: Purl.

Work 8 rows in stripe pattern.

Now complete as for Right gloves.

to finish
Extra-long gloves

Thread ribbon from the side seam through every two stitches on the row before the thumb shaping starts, securing with a knot at the side seam.

Cosy mittens

These mittens will keep your hands warm and look fabulous. Add beads and sequins to dazzle, fabulous flowers for little girls and pink hearts to say I love you.

Materials

• Customized mittens

One 50 g (2 oz) ball of Rowan Kid Classic in silver (840 Crystal)

Silver lurex, for knitting and embroidery

Pair of 4.5 mm (US 7) knitting needles

Clear glass beads and selection of silver sequins

• Two-colour mittens

One 50 g (2 oz) ball of Rowan Kid Classic in each of the following colours: pink (819 Pinched) and purple (844 Flirty)

Pair of 4.5 mm (US 7) knitting needles

• Plain mittens

One 50 g (2 oz) ball of Rowan Kid Classic in red (847 Cherry Red)

2 flowers

Pair of 4.5 mm (US 7) knitting needles

Sizes

* Small (to fit child aged 5–10 years)
* Medium (to fit an average adult female hand)

Tension

20 sts x 28 rows to 10 cm (4 in) square measured over st-st using 4.5 mm (US 7) knitting needles

Abbreviations

alt alternate; **cont** continu(e)(ing); **dec** decreas(e)(ing)ing; **foll(s)** follow(s)(ing); **inc** increas(e)(ing); **K** knit; **K2tog** knit 2 stitches together; **M1** make 1 stitch; **P** purl; **rem** remain(ing); **RS** right side; **st(s)** stitch(es); **st-st** stocking stitch; **tbl** through back of loop; **WS** wrong side

Designer's note

This is an ideal glove project for a beginner as there is only the thumb to work. These mittens are so quick to knit you will have them finished and be wearing them in no time. To keep your mittens safe (and this is not just for children!) make a length of twisted cord from any leftover yarn (see page 33), attach a mitten to each end and thread through coat sleeves.

Working instructions

Pattern is written for the Customized mittens in two sizes: small size first with medium size in brackets. For the Two-colour mittens, work right hand in pink and left hand in purple. Work the Plain mittens in one colour throughout.

The gloves

to make

Customized mittens right glove

Using 4.5 mm (US 7) knitting needles and silver lurex, cast on 34(38) sts.

Rib row 1: [K2, P2] to last 2 sts, K2.

Rib row 2: [P2, K2] to last 2 sts, P2.

These 2 rows form the rib pattern.

Change to main shade and work a further 14(18) rows in rib.

Next row (RS): Knit.

Next row: Purl.

These last 2 rows form st-st.

Work a further 2(4) rows in st-st.**

Shape thumb

Row 1 (RS): K17(19), M1, K3, M1, K14(16). 36(40) sts.

Work 3 rows in st-st.

Row 5 (RS): K17(19), M1, K5, M1, K14(16). 38(42) sts.

Next row: Purl.

Cont to inc as above on next row and every foll alt row to 42(48) sts.

Next row: Purl.

Knit thumb

Next row (RS): K28(32), turn.

Next row: P11(13).

***Working on these 11(13) sts only, work 10(12) rows in st-st.

Next row (dec): K1, K2 tog to end. 6(7) sts.

Break off yarn, run yarn through rem sts, draw up and fasten off. Join thumb seam.

With RS facing, rejoin yarn, pick up and K2 sts at base of thumb, then K to end. 33(37) sts.

Next row: Purl.

Work 16(22) rows in st-st.

Shape top

Row 1 (RS) (dec): K1, [K2tog tbl, K11(13), K2tog, K1] twice. 29(33) sts.

Row 2: Purl.

Row 3 (RS) (dec): K1, [K2tog tbl, K9(11), K2tog, K1] twice. 25(29) sts.

Row 4: Purl.

Cont to dec on next row and every foll alt row to 21 sts.

Cast off.

Customized mittens left glove

Work as for Right hand to **.

Shape thumb

Row 1 (RS): K14(16), M1, K3, M1, K17(19). 36(40) sts.

Work 3 rows in st-st.

Row 5 (RS): K14(16), M1, K5, M1, K17(19). 38(42) sts.

Work 1 row in st-st.

Cont to inc as above on next row and every foll alt row to 42(48) sts.

Next row: Purl.

Knit thumb

Next row (RS): K25(29), turn.

Next row: P11(13).

Now complete as for Right hand from ***.

to finish

Customized mittens

Before customizing, press the knitting as described on the ball band. Using the photograph as a guide, embroider stars on the thumb and back of the mittens using silver lurex. Sew on glass beads and sequins randomly. Sew seams together using mattress stitch (or back stitch if preferred).

Two-colour mittens

With the back of the right-hand mitten facing and using the opposite colour yarn, embroider heart motifs using the Swiss darning technique (see page 34). Start at the central stitch and six rows up work the motif as shown on the chart for the right-hand mitten.

Work the embroidery on the left-hand mitten following the chart for the left-hand mitten. Sew the seams together using mattress stitch (or back stitch if preferred).

Plain mittens

Sew the seams together using mattress stitch (or back stitch if preferred).
Using 4.5 mm (US 7) needles and contrast shade, make two knitted flowers as described on page 36. Sew seams together and stitch into place.

All mittens

Add twisted cord (optional).

2-colour mittens

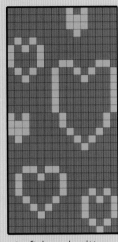 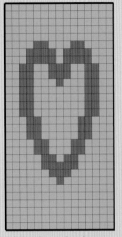

Left-hand mitten   Right-hand mitten

Toasty tweed

Whether in funky stripes or manly tweeds, these gloves will stop you freezing in winter. Wrap your hands around a steaming drink for extra warmth.

Materials

- **Stripy gloves**

    One 50 g (2 oz) ball of Rowan Yorkshire Tweed DK in each of the following colours: A red (344 Scarlet), B purple (342 Revel), C lime (349 Frog), D pink (350 Frolic) and E aqua (347 Skip)

    Pair of 3.75 mm (US 5) knitting needles

    Pair of 4 mm (US 6) knitting needles

- **Plain gloves**

    Two 50 g (2 oz) balls of Rowan Yorkshire Tweed DK in navy (346 Champion)

    Pair of 3.75 mm (US 5) knitting needles

    Pair of 4 mm (US 6) knitting needles

Sizes

- Medium (to fit an average adult female hand)
- Large (to fit an average adult male hand)

Tension

22 sts x 30 rows to 10 cm (4 in) square measured over st-st using 4 mm (US 6) knitting needles

Abbreviations

cont continu(e)(ing); **dec** decreas(e)(ing); **foll(s)** follow(s)(ing); **inc** increas(e)(ing); **K** knit; **K2tog** knit 2 stitches together; **M1** make 1 stitch; **P** purl; **rem** remain(ing); **RS** right side; **st(s)** stitch(es); **st-st** stocking stitch; **WS** wrong side

Designer's note

These gloves are really funky, with the fingers knitted in different colours. You can experiment with your own colour combinations: perhaps variations of one shade such as reds and pinks, blues and greens. You could even include different textures of yarn – be experimental.

Working instructions

The pattern is written for the Stripy gloves in two sizes: medium first with large in brackets. Work the Plain gloves in the appropriate size but in one colour throughout.

The gloves
to make
Stripy gloves right glove

Using 3.75 mm (US 5) knitting needles and yarn A, cast on 38(42) sts.

Rib row 1: [K2, P2] to last 2 sts, K2.

Rib row 2: [P2, K2] to last 2 sts, P2.

These 2 rows set the rib pattern.

Work 21(25) more rows in rib, ending with a RS row.

Next row (WS) (dec): [P2, K2] 8(9) times, K2 tog, P2, rib to end. 37(41) sts.

Change to 4 mm (US 6) knitting needles and work in stripe pattern for hand of glove as folls:

2 rows B, 1 row A, 2 rows C, 1 row D, 1 row E, 2 rows B, 1 row A, 1 row D, 3 rows A, 1 row C, 2 rows E, 2 rows D, 1 row B, 1 row A, 1 row C, 2 rows D, 2 rows A, 1 row E, 2 rows B, 1 row D, 2 rows C, 2 rows A.

Beginning with a K row, work first 4 rows of stripe pattern in st st**.

Shape thumb

Continue in stripe pattern.

Row 1 (RS): K19(22), M1, K3(1), M1, K15(18). 39(43) sts.

Work 3 rows in stripe pattern.

Row 5 (RS): K19(22), M1, K5(3), M1, K15(18). 41(45) sts.

Work 3 rows in stripe pattern.

Cont to inc as above on next row and every foll 4th row to 47(53) sts.

Next row: Purl.

Knit thumb

Next row (RS): Using yarn D, K32(36), turn, cast on 1 st.

Next row: P12(14), turn, cast on 1 st.

Change to yarn B and, working on these 13(15) sts
only, work 14(18) rows.

Next row (dec): K1, (K2tog) to end.

7(8) sts.

Break off yarn, run yarn through rem sts, draw up and
fasten off.

Join thumb seam.

With RS facing and yarn D, rejoin yarn, pick up and
knit 2 sts from base of thumb and K to end.

38(42) sts.

Next row: Purl.

Work 8(10) rows in stripe pattern, keeping stripe
sequence correct.

Knit first finger***

Next row (RS): Using yarn A, K24(27), turn, cast on
1 st.

Next row: P11(13), turn, cast on 1 st.

12(14) sts.

Change to yarn D and, working on these 12(14) sts
only, work 20(22) rows.

Next row (dec): [K2tog] to end. 6(7) sts.

Break off yarn, run yarn through rem sts, draw up and
fasten off.

Join finger seam.

Knit second finger

With RS facing and using yarn A, rejoin yarn, pick up
and knit 2 sts from base of finger, K4(5) sts, turn, cast
on 1 st.

Next row: P11(13) sts, turn, cast on 1 st. 12(14) sts.

Change to yarn E and, working on these 12(14) sts only,
work 24(26) rows.

Next row (dec): [K2tog] to end. 6(7) sts.

Break off yarn, run yarn through rem sts, draw up and
fasten off.

Join finger seam.

Knit third finger

With RS facing and yarn A, rejoin yarn, pick up and knit 2 sts from base of finger, K4(5) sts, turn, cast on 1 st.

Next row: P11(13), turn, cast on 1 st. 12(14) sts. Change to yarn C and, working on these 12(14) sts only, work 20(22) rows.

Next row (dec): [K2tog] to end. 6(7) sts.

Break off yarn, run yarn through rem sts, draw up and fasten off.

Join finger seam.

Knit fourth finger

With RS facing and yarn A, rejoin yarn, pick up and knit 0(2) sts from base of finger, K6(4), M0(1) K0(1). 12(13) sts.

Next row: P12(12), M0(1), P0(1). Change to yarn D and working on these 12(14) sts only, work 14(16) rows.

Next row (dec): [K2tog] to end. 6(7) sts.

Break off yarn, run yarn through rem sts, draw up and fasten off.

Sew finger and side seams using mattress stitch on RS to match stripes neatly (or back stitch if preferred).

Stripy gloves left glove

Work as for Right glove to **.

Shape thumb

Row 1 (RS): K15(18), M1, K3(1), M1, K19(22).
39(43) sts.

Work 3 rows in stripe pattern.

Row 5 (RS): K15(18), M1, K5(3), M1, K19(22).
41(45) sts.

Work 3 rows in stripe pattern.

Cont to inc as above on next row and every foll 4th
row to 47(53) sts.

Next row: Purl.

Knit thumb

Next row (RS): Using yarn D, K28(32), turn, cast on
1(1) st.

Next row: P12(14), turn, cast on 1(1) st.

Change to yarn E and, working on these 13(15) sts
only, work 14(18) rows.

Next row (dec): K1, [K2tog] to end. 7(8) sts.

Break off yarn, run yarn through rem sts, draw up
and fasten off.

Join thumb seam.

With RS facing and yarn D, rejoin yarn, pick up and
knit 2 sts from base of thumb and K to end. 38(42) sts.

Next row: Purl.

Work 8(10) rows in stripe pattern, keeping stripe
sequence correct.

Now complete as for Right glove from ***, working
first finger in yarn B, second finger in yarn D, third
finger in yarn E and fourth finger in yarn C.

Classic elegance

Inspired by a golden vintage era when ladies
always wore gloves, these classic styles show
that elegance never goes out of fashion.

Materials

- **Lace-edged gloves**

  Two 50 g (2 oz) balls of Jaeger Matchmaker Merino 4-ply in
  soft green (715 Thyme)

  Pair of 2.75 mm (US 2) knitting needles

- **Plain gloves**

  Two 50 g balls (2 oz) of Jaeger Matchmaker Merino 4-ply in
  soft blue (748 Dewberry)

  Pair of 2.75 mm (US 2) knitting needles

Sizes

- One size (to fit an average adult female hand)

Tension

32 sts x 40 rows to 10 cm (4 in) square measured over st-st
using 2.75 mm (US 2) knitting needles

Abbreviations

cont continu(e)(ing); **dec** decreas(e)(ing); **foll(s)**
follow(s)(ing); **inc** increase; **K** knit; **K2tog** knit 2 stitches
together; **LH** left-hand; **M1** make 1 stitch; **P** purl; **P2tog** purl 2
stitches together; **rem** remain(ing); **rep** repeat; **RH** right-
hand; **RS** right side; **st(s)** stitch(es); **st-st** stocking stitch; **tbl**
through back of loop; **WS** wrong side; **yo** yarn over

Designer's note

These gloves are simply elegant. I have knitted them in a soft
merino 4-ply, but they could be knitted in any 4-ply yarn:
alpaca, cashmere, angora or silk. The gloves will make a
beautiful addition to a winter wardrobe, whether for yourself
or as a gift.

The gloves

to make

Lace-edged gloves right glove

Using 2.75 mm (US 2) knitting needles, work picot cast-on as folls:
*Cast on 5 sts, cast off 2 sts, slip st on RH needle back onto LH
needle* (3 sts now on LH needle), rep from * to * until 66 sts on
needle, cast on 1 st. (67 sts)

Row 1: Knit.

Row 2: Knit.

Row 3 (dec): K1, (K2tog tbl, K9, K2tog) 5 times, K1. (57 sts)

Row 4: Purl.

Row 5 (dec): K1, (K2tog tbl, K7, K2tog) 5 times, K1. (47 sts)

Row 6: Purl.

Row 7 (inc): K1, (K2tog tbl, [yo, K1] 5 times, yo, K2tog) 5 times,
K1. (67 sts)

Row 8: Knit.

Work last 6 rows once more.

Work row 3 once more. (57 sts)

Next row (WS) (dec): P27, P2tog, P28. (56 sts)

Rib row 1 (RS): [K2, P2] to end.

Rib row 2: [P2, K2] to end.

Work 28 more rows in rib.

Starting with a knit row, work 8 rows in st-st.**

Lace-edged gloves left glove

Work as for Lace-edged glove right glove to **.

Plain gloves right glove

Using 2.75 mm (US 2) knitting needles, cast on 56 sts. Then
continue as for the Lace-edged glove.

Plain gloves left glove

Work as for Plain gloves left glove to **

Both right gloves

Shape thumb

Row 1 (RS): K29, M1, K4, M1, K23. 58 sts.

Work 3 rows in st-st.

Row 5 (RS): K29, M1, K6, M1, K23. 60 sts.

Work 3 rows in st-st.

Cont to inc as above on next row and every foll 4th row to 68 sts.

Work 3 rows in st-st.

Knit thumb

Next row (RS): K46, turn, cast on 2 sts.

Next row: P20, turn, cast on 2 sts. 22 sts.

***Working on these 22 sts only, work 20 rows in st-st.

Next row (RS) (dec): K2, [K2tog, K2] 5 times. 17 sts.

Next row: Purl.

Next row (dec): K1, [K2tog] to end. 9 sts.

Break off yarn, run yarn through rem sts, draw up and fasten off. Join thumb seam.

With RS facing, rejoin yarn, pick up and knit 6 sts from base of thumb and K to end. 56 sts.

Next row: Purl.

Work 16 rows in st-st.

Knit first finger

Next row (RS): K36, turn, cast on 1 st.

Next row: P17, turn, cast on 1 st. 18 sts.

Working on these 18 sts only, work 24 rows in st-st.

Next row (RS) (dec): K2, [K2tog, K2] 4 times. 14 sts.

Next row: Purl.

Next row (dec): [K2tog] to end. 7 sts.

Break off yarn, run yarn through rem sts, draw up and fasten off. Join finger seam.

Knit second finger

With RS facing, rejoin yarn, pick up, knit 2 sts from base of finger, K7 sts, turn, cast on 1 st.

Next row: P17, turn cast on 1 st. 18 sts. Working on these 18 sts only, work 28 rows in st-st.

Next row (RS) (dec): K2, [K2tog, K2] 4 times. 14 sts.

Next row: Purl.

Next row (dec): [K2tog] to end. 7 sts.

Break off yarn, run yarn through rem sts, draw up and fasten off. Join finger seam.

Knit third finger

With RS facing, rejoin yarn, pick up, knit 2 sts from base of finger, K7 sts, turn, cast on 1 st.

Next row: P17, turn, cast on 1 st. 18 sts.

Working on these 18 sts only, work 24 rows in st-st.

Next row (RS) (dec): K2, [K2tog, K2] 4 times. 14 sts.

Next row: Purl.

Next row (dec): [K2tog] to end. 7 sts.

Break off yarn, run yarn through rem sts, draw up and fasten off. Join finger seam.

Knit fourth finger

With RS facing, rejoin yarn, pick up and knit 4 sts from base of third finger, K to end.

Next row: Purl.

Working on these 16 sts only, work 20 rows in st-st.

Next row (RS) (dec): [K2tog, K2] 4 times. 12 sts.

Next row: Purl.

Next row (dec): [K2tog] to end. 6 sts.

Break off yarn, run yarn through rem sts, draw up and fasten off. Sew finger and side seams using mattress stitch (or back stitch if preferred).

Both left gloves

Shape thumb

Row 1 (RS): K23, M1, K4, M1, K29. 58sts.

Work 3 rows in st-st.

Row 5 (RS): K23, M1, K6, M1, K29. 60 sts.

Work 3 rows in st-st.

Cont to inc as above on next row and every foll 4th row to 68 sts.

Work 3 rows in st-st.

Knit thumb

Next row (RS): K40, turn, cast on 2 sts.

Next row: P20, turn, cast on 2 sts. (22 sts)

Complete to match Right glove from ***.

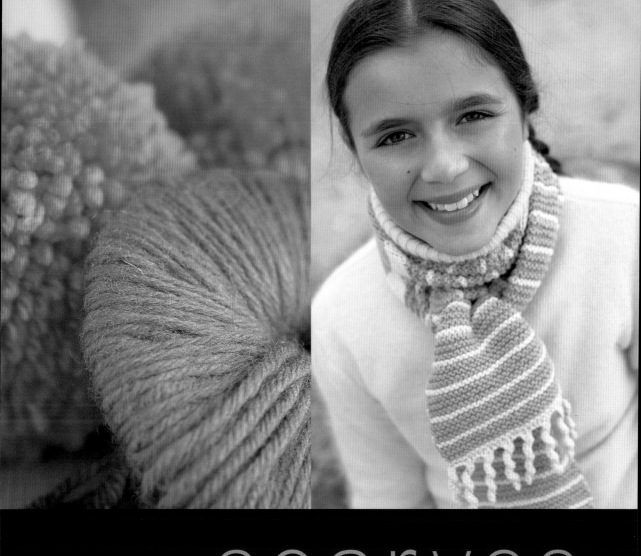

scarves

Rainbow rib

Wrap these extra-long scarves round and round to keep you snug and warm as you battle windy winter mornings.

Materials

- **Striped scarf**

  Two 100 g (4 oz) balls of Rowan Chunky Print in each of the following colours: A beige (072 Native) and B brown (080 Pit)

  Pair of 8 mm (US 11) knitting needles

- **Plain scarf**

  Three 100 g (4 oz) balls of Rowan Chunky Print in red/grey marl (075 Swizzle)

  Pair of 8 mm (US 11) knitting needles

Sizes

- One size: 23 x 200 cm (9 x 79 in) approximately

Tension

11 sts x 16 rows to 10 cm (4 in) square measured over st-st using 8 mm (US 11) knitting needles

Abbreviations

cont continu(e)(ing); **foll(s)** follow(s)(ing); **K** knit; **P** purl; **RS** right side; **st(s)** stitch(es); **st-st** stocking stitch

Designer's note

This scarf pattern is an updated classic. I have made it extra-long so that it can be wound round and round to keep out even the bitterest chill. Be inventive with your colour choices for the stripes, or use up oddments of yarn.

If you only have fine yarns, use use two or more strands of different colours to get the correct weight.

Working instructions

The pattern is written for the Striped scarf. Work the Plain scarf in the same way but in one colour throughout.

The scarves

to make

Striped scarf

Using 8 mm (US 11) knitting needles and yarn A, cast on 27 sts.

Work in rib, setting sts as folls:

Row 1 (RS): K6, [P5, K5] twice, K1.

Row 2: K1, [P5, K5] twice, P5, K1.

These 2 rows form the rib pattern.

Work 8 more rows in rib.

Change to yarn B.

Work 10 rows in rib.

These 20 rows form the rib and stripe pattern. Cont to work in 20-row stripe repeat until scarf measures approximately 200 cm (79 in), ending with yarn B.

Cast off in rib.

Pom pom party

The pom poms on these scarves take on a life and movement of their own, almost as if dancing – watch out, or you'll be boogie-ing at the bus stop!

Materials

- **Ribbed scarf**

  Four 50 g (2 oz) balls of Jaeger Matchmaker Merino DK in cream (662 Cream)

  Pair of 4 mm (US 6) knitting needles

  Ten 4.5 cm (1¾ in) pompoms

- **Pom pom scarf**

  One 50 g (2 oz) ball of Debbie Bliss DK in each of the following colours: blue (201), red (700), pink (703), orange (701) and butter (504)

  Three 7 cm (2¾ in) pompoms in each colour

Sizes

- **Ribbed scarf**

  20 x 140 cm (8 x 55 in) approximately

- **Pom pom scarf**

  7 x 125 cm (2¾ x 49 in) approximately

Tension

22 sts x 30 rows to 10 cm (4 in) square measured over st-st using 4 mm (US 6) knitting needles

Abbreviations

cont continu(e)(ing); **foll(s)** follow(s)(ing); **K** knit; **P** purl; **RS** right side; **st-st** stocking stitch

Designer's note

This scarf pattern has two very different options. One is a classic rib scarf with pom poms attached at each end; the other is a scarf made entirely from pom poms joined together – an ideal beginner's project.

The scarves

to make

Ribbed scarf

Using 4 mm (US 6) knitting needles, cast on 46 sts.

Work in rib, setting sts as folls:

Row 1 (RS): K1 [P2, K5] 6 times, P2, K1.

Row 2: K1 [K2, P5] 6 times, K3.

These 2 rows set the rib pattern.

Cont to work in rib until scarf measures
approximately 140 cm (55 in).

Cast off in rib.

Pom pom scarf

Make a 7 cm (3 in) pom pom as described on page
32. Secure with a knitted cord, leaving the ends
loose.

*Make the next 7 cm (3 in) pom pom and secure
using the ends from the first knitted cord. Join in
another knitted cord, leaving the ends loose.

Repeat from * 13 more times to make a scarf of 15
pom poms joined together.

to finish
Ribbed scarf

Make ten 4.5 cm (2 in) pom poms as described on page 32 and attach five to each end of the scarf with a knitted cord.

Divine lace

Whether you are nine or ninety, this is the prettiest of scarves. Delicate, wispy lace stitches envelope you in soft yarns, making you feel truly divine.

Materials

- **Narrow scarf**
  Three 25 g (1 oz) balls of Rowan Yorkshire Tweed 4-ply in blue (267 Sheer)
  Pair of 5 mm (US 8) knitting needles

- **Wide scarf**
  Two 25 g (1 oz) balls of Rowan Kid Silk Haze in pink (606 Candy Girl)
  Pair of 4 mm (US 6) knitting needles

Sizes

- Narrow scarf 15 x 160 cm (6 x 63 in) approximately
- Wide scarf 30 x 160 cm (12 x 63 in) approximately

Tension

- Yorkshire Tweed 4-ply
  22 sts x 24 rows to 10 cm (4 in) square measured over lace pattern using 5 mm (US 8) knitting needles
- Kid Silk Haze
  22 sts x 28 rows to 10 cm (4 in) square measured over lace pattern using 4 mm (US 6) knitting needles

Abbreviations

foll(s) follow(s)(ing); **garter st** garter stitch; **K** knit; **K2tog** knit 2 stitches together; **LH** left-hand; **P** purl; **psso** pass slipped stitch over; **rep** repeat; **RH** right-hand; **RS** right side; **sl1** slip 1 stitch; **st(s)** stitch(es); **tbl** through back of loop **yo** yarn over

Designer's note

The wide lacy scarf knitted in silk and mohair feels fabulous – like wearing a feather. The tweed yarn is knitted on a bigger needle than usual so that the scarf grows really quickly. If the tweed feels a little prickly, hand wash the finished scarf in some fabric conditioner. This will not only make the scarf soft but will also felt the fabric slightly, making it extra snug.

Working instructions

The pattern is written for the Narrow scarf first with the Wide scarf in brackets.

The scarves
to make

Using 5(4) mm (US 8(6)) knitting needles, work picot cast-on as folls:

Cast on 5 sts, cast off 2 sts, slip st on RH needle back onto LH needle (3 sts now on LH needle). Rep from * to * until 33(63) sts on needle, cast on 1 st. 34(64) sts.

Knit 4 rows (garter st).

Work lace pattern

Row 1(RS): K2, [K2, K2tog, yo, K2tog but do not slip from needle, knit the first of these 2 sts again, then slip both sts from needle together, yo, sl1, K1, psso, K2] 3(6) times, K2.

Row 2: K2, P30(60), K2.

Row 3: K2, [K1, K2tog, yo, K4, yo, sl1, K1, psso, K1] 3(6) times, K2.

Row 4: K2, P30(60), K2.

Row 5: K2, [K2tog, yo, K1, K2tog, (yo) twice, sl1, K1, psso, K1, yo, sl1, K1, psso] 3(6) times, K2.

Row 6: K2, [P4, K1 into first yo, P1 into 2nd yo, P4] 3(6) times, K2.

Row 7: K2, [K2, yo, sl1, K1, psso, K2, K2tog, yo, K2] 3(6) times, K2.

Row 8: K2, P30(60), K2.

Row 9: K2, [K3, yo, sl1, K1, psso, K2tog, yo, K3] 3(6) times, K2.

Row 10: K2, P30(60), K2.

Rep these 10 rows of lace pattern until work measures approx 160 cm (63 in) from start, ending with row 2 of lace pattern.

Knit 4 rows (garter st).

Work picot cast-off as folls:

Cast off 3 sts, *slip st on RH needle back onto LH needle, cast on 2 sts using cable method, then cast off 5 sts, rep from * to end.

On the fringe

This all-over fringed scarf is a playful design, and a dramatic entrance is guaranteed. For a subtler effect, add fringes at each end only.

Materials

- **Scarf with all-over fringing**

  Three 50 g (1 oz) balls of Jaeger Extra Fine Merino Chunky in blue (012 Blue Bird) and two 50 g (2 oz) balls of the same yarn in blue marl (013 Blue Fan), for fringing

  Pair of 6 mm (US 10) knitting needles

- **Scarf with fringe edging**

  Four 50 g (1 oz) balls of Jaeger Extra Fine Merino Chunky in grey marl (019 Gravel)

  Pair of 6 mm (US 10) knitting needles

Sizes

- One size 18 x 140 cm (7 x 55 in) approximately

Tension

16 sts x 20 rows to 10 cm (4 in) square measured over st-st using 6 mm (US 10) knitting needles

Abbreviations

cont continu(e)(ing); **foll(s)** follow(s)(ing); **K** knit; **P** purl; **rep** repeat; **RS** right side; **st(s)** stitch(es); **st-st** stocking stitch; **WS** wrong side

Designer's note

This scarf has been designed to show how a classic pattern can be transformed just by adding fringing in different ways. I have made one version really fun by adding fringing along the whole length of the scarf. This will keep you extra warm – perhaps an ideal scarf for that winter skiing trip?

The scarves

to make

Using 6 mm (US 10) knitting needles, cast on 29 sts.

Work in moss st, setting sts as folls:

Row 1 (RS): [K1, P1] to last st, K1.

Row 2: [K1, P1] to last st, K1.

Work 2 more rows in moss st.

Now work 20-row pattern rep as folls:

Row 1: K1, P1 K25, P1, K1.

Row 2: K1, P1, K1, P23, K1, P1, K1.

Work these 2 rows 7 times more.

Row 17: As row 1.

Row 18: [K1, P1] to last st, K1.

Work 2 more rows in moss st.

Cont to work in 20-row pattern rep until scarf measures approximately 140 cm (55 in), ending with row 20.

Work 1 more row in moss st.

Cast off knitwise on WS.

to finish

Scarf with all-over fringing

Cut 10 cm (4 in) lengths of yarn. With the reverse side of the scarf facing and using the photograph as a guide, thread a single length through every other reverse stitch along the width of the scarf on rows 1 and 2 of the moss stitch after the cast-on, and then on every rows 18 and 19 of the 20-row pattern repeat. When half the scarf is complete, repeat the fringing, starting at the other end of the scarf. When the fringe is complete, trim the ends.

Scarf with fringe edging

For each fringe, cut three 20 cm (8 in) lengths of yarn. Fold a strand in half and draw the folded end through a stitch at the bottom edge of the scarf. Draw the loose ends of the yarn through the loop and pull firmly to form a knot. Repeat along the width of the scarf. When the fringe is complete, trim the ends. Make another fringe in the same way along the top edge of the scarf.

Just for him

This scarf uses the finest ingredients, mixing a classic stitch with a beautiful cashmere yarn. Just add a dashing man.

Materials

Three 100 g (4 oz) balls of Debbie Bliss Cashmerino Superchunky in olive (017)

Pair of 7 mm (US 10½) knitting needles

Sizes

• One size 20 x 130 cm (8 x 51 in) approximately

Tension

12 sts x 20 rows to 10 cm (4 in) square measured over moss stitch using 7 mm (US 10½) knitting needles

Abbreviations

cont continu(e)(ing); **K** knit; **moss st** moss stitch; **P** purl; **rep** repeat; **RS** right side; **st(s)** stitch(es); **st-st** stocking stitch; **WS** wrong side

Designer's note

This scarf has been designed with a rugged outdoors type of guy in mind. The simple stitch and chunky yarn all add to its masculine appeal, and yet it is knitted in the softest of cashmere blends. As we all know, the more rugged the outside, the softer the inside.

The scarf

to make

Using 7 mm (US 10½) knitting needles, cast on 25 sts.

Work in moss st, setting sts as folls:

Row 1 (RS): [K1, P1] to last st, K1.

Row 2: [K1, P1] to last st, K1.

Cont to work in moss stitch until scarf measures approximately 130 cm (51 in), ending with a RS row. Cast off knitwise on WS.

Pockets of charm

This is the perfect scarf for windy days, when you want to keep your hands bare for kite flying or eating hot chestnuts in the park.

Materials

- **Contrast-colour scarf**

  One 100 g (4 oz) ball of Rowan Big Wool in A orange (015 Pip) and three 100 g (4 oz) balls of the same yarn in colour B red marl (128 Bohemian)

  Pair of 10 mm (US 15) knitting needles

- **Striped scarf**

  One 100 g (4 oz) ball of Rowan Big Wool in each of the following colours: A sky (026 Blue Velvet), B blue marl (021 Ice Blue) and C navy (032 Rascal)

  Pair of 10 mm (US 15) knitting needles

Sizes

- Medium (to fit child aged 5–10 years)

  18 x 140 cm (7 x 55 in) approximately

- Large (to fit an average adult female)

  23.5 x 176 cm (9½ x 69 in) approximately

Tension

9 sts x 13 rows to 10 cm (4 in) square measured over st-st using 10 mm (US 15) knitting needles

Abbreviations

cont continu(e)(ing); **foll(s)** follow(s)(ing); **K** knit; **moss st** moss stitch; **P** purl; **RS** right side; **st(s)** stitch(es); **st-st** stocking stitch; **WS** wrong side

Designer's note

If you want a perfect fit for your pocket scarf, get a friend to measure you. You will need to find the length from the centre back of your neck to the tip of your middle finger with your arm slightly bent. Double this measurement to give you the ideal length for your scarf.

Working instructions

Pattern is written for medium size first with large scarf in brackets.

The scarves

to make

Contrast-colour scarf

Make first pocket front

Using 10 mm (US 15) knitting needles and yarn A, cast on 17(21) sts.

Work in moss st as folls:

Row 1 (RS): [K1, P1] 8(10) times, K1.

Row 2: [K1, P1] 8(10) times, K1.

Work these 2 rows once more.

Row 5: K1, P1, K13(17), P1, K1.

Row 6: K1, P1, K1, P11(15), K1, P1, K1.

These 2 rows form the pattern. Work a further 14(20) rows, ending with a WS row.

Work 3 rows in moss st, ending with RS row.

Next row: Knit (fold line).

Work the scarf (RS of pocket now becomes WS of scarf)

Row 1 (WS): K1, P1, K1, P11(15), K1, P1, K1.

Row 2 (RS): K1, P1, K13(17), P1, K1.

Change to yarn B and cont to work in pattern as set until scarf (excluding pocket front) measures approximately 140 cm (55 in)(176 cm (70 in)), ending with a WS row.

Change to yarn A and work 2 rows.

Make second pocket front (RS of scarf now becomes WS of pocket)

Next row: Purl (fold line).

Work 3 rows in moss st, ending with a RS row.

Row 5: K1, P1, K13(17), P1, K1.

Row 6: K1, P1, K1, P11(15), K1, P1, K1.

Work a further 14(20) rows, ending with a RS row.

Work 4 rows in moss st, ending with a RS row.

Cast off knitwise.

Striped scarf

Make first pocket front

Using 10 mm (US 15) knitting needles and yarn A, cast on 17(21) sts.

Work in moss st as folls:

Row 1 (RS): [K1, P1] 8(10) times, K1.

Row 2: [K1, P1] 8(10) times, K1.

Work these 2 rows once more.

Row 5: K1, P1, K13(17), P1, K1.

Row 6: K1, P1, K1, P11(15), K1, P1, K1.

These 2 rows form the pattern. Work a further 14(20) rows, ending with a WS row.

Work 3 rows in moss st, ending with a RS row.

Next row: Knit (fold line).

Work the scarf (RS of pocket now becomes WS of scarf)

Row 1 (WS): K1, P1, K1, P11(15), K1, P1, K1.

Row 2 (RS): K1, P1, K13(17), P1, K1.

Work a further 26(32) rows, ending with a WS row.

Now work in the following stripe sequence:

4 rows B, 4 rows C, 4 rows B, 4 rows A.

Cont in stripe sequence until scarf (excluding pocket front) measures approximately 120 cm (47½ in)(150 cm (59 in)).

Change to yarn C and cont to work a further 26(32) rows in pattern, ending with a WS row.

Make second pocket front (RS of scarf now becomes WS of pocket)

Next row: Purl (fold line).

Work 3 rows in moss st, ending with a RS row.

Row 5: K1, P1, K13(17), P1, K1.

Row 6: K1, P1, K1, P11(15), K1, P1, K1.

Work a further 14(20) rows, ending with a RS row.

Work 4 rows in moss st, ending with a RS row.

Cast off knitwise.

to finish

Contrast-colour scarf

Fold the first pocket front back onto the scarf at the fold line.

Stitch into place RS using back stitch, one stitch in from the edge.

Striped scarf

Repeat for the second pocket front.

Follow the instructions for the Contrast-colour scarf.

Beautifully beaded

This elegant scarf will shimmer in the winter sunshine. You'll look glamorous throughout the day and sparkle well into the night.

Materials

Five 50 g (2 oz) balls of Jaeger Matchmaker Merino Aran in lilac (772 Clover)

Approximately 1400 clear glass beads

Pair of 4.5 mm (US 7) knitting needles

Sizes

• One size 18 x 140 cm (7 x 55 in) approximately

Tension

19 sts x 25 rows to 10 cm (4 in) square measured over st-st using 4.5 mm (US 7) knitting needles

Abbreviations

K knit; **LH** left-hand; **P** purl; **RS** right side; **st(s)** stitch(es); **st-st** stocking stitch; **WS** wrong side

Special abbreviation B1 Bead one – place a bead by bringing yarn to front (RS) of work and slipping a bead up next to st just worked, slip st purlwise from LH needle to RH needle and take yarn to back (WS) of work, leaving bead sitting in front of slipped st on RS.

Designer's note

This is a beautiful, elegant scarf that shimmers. Working with beads is a very rewarding and effective way of adding interest to your knitting, but it does require a little preparation. Before starting to knit, thread beads onto the yarn. To do this, thread a fine sewing needle with sewing thread. Knot the ends of the thread together and then pass the end of the yarn through this loop. Thread a bead onto the sewing thread and gently slide it along onto knitting yarn. Continue in this way until you have the required number of beads threaded on the yarn.

The scarf

to make

Using 4.5 mm (US 7) knitting needles, cast on 35 sts.

Row 1 (RS): Knit.

Row 2: Knit.

Row 3: [K1, B1] to last st, K1.

Row 4 and every alt row: K2, P31, K2.

Row 5: K1, [K1, B1] to last 2 sts, K2.

Row 7: [K1, B1] to last st, K1.

Row 9: K2, [B1, K9] 3 times, B1, K2.

Row 11: K3, [B1, K7, B1, K1] 3 times, K2.

Row 13: K4, [B1, K5, B1, K3] 3 times, K1.

Row 15: K5, [B1, K3, B1, K5] 3 times.

Row 17: K6, [B1, K1, B1, K7] twice, B1, K1, B1, K6.

Row 19: K7, [B1, K9] twice, B1, K7.

Row 20: K2, P31, K2.

The last 12 rows (row 9 to row 20) form the beaded chevron pattern.

Rep these 12 rows 31 times more, ending with a WS row.

Next row: [K1, B1] to last st, K1.

Next row: K2, P31, K2.

Next row: K1, [K1, B1] to last 2 sts, K2.

Next row: K2, P31, K2.

Next row: [K1, B1] to last st, K1.

Next row: Knit.

Next row: Knit.

Cast off knitwise on WS.

to finish

For each fringe, cut one 15 cm (6 in) length of yarn and thread on four beads. Slip two beads to each end and tie a knot. Fold the strand in half and draw the folded end through a stitch at the bottom edge of the scarf, draw the loose ends of the yarn through the loop and pull firmly to form a knot. Repeat along the width of the scarf to complete the fringe. Make a beaded fringe in the same way along the top edge of the scarf.

Snuggle scarf

Wrap yourself and your loved ones in one of these gorgeously snug scarves and really enjoy those cold, crisp, frosty mornings.

Materials

- **Three-colour scarf**

    Two 50 g (2 oz) balls of Rowan Calmer in each of the following colours: A berry (469 Amour), B pink (477 Blush) and C red (476 Coral)

    Pair of 5 mm (US 8) knitting needles

- **Plain scarf**

    Three 50 g (2 oz) balls of Rowan Calmer in navy (479 Slosh)

    Pair of 5 mm (US 8) knitting needles

- **Four-colour scarf with curly edging**

    One 50 g (2 oz) ball of Rowan Calmer in each of the following colours: A baby pink (470 Flamingo), B lilac (462 Chiffon), C sky (463 Calmer) and D lime (464 Laurel)

    Pair of 5 mm (US 8) knitting needles

Sizes

- Small (Four-colour scarf)

    14.5 x 130 cm (5¾ x 51 in) approximately

- Medium (Plain scarf)

    17 x 130 cm (6¾ x 51 in) approximately

- Large (3-colour scarf)

    17 x 180 cm (6¾ x 71 in) approximately

Tension

21 sts x 30 rows to 10 cm (4 in) square measured over st-st using 5 mm (US 8) knitting needles

Abbreviations

foll(s) follow(s)(ing); **garter st** garter stitch; **K** knit; **LH** left-hand; **P** purl; **rep** repeat; **RS** right side; **st(s)** stitch(es); **st-st** stocking stitch; **WS** wrong side

Designer's note

This is the ideal knitting project for a beginner. The simple pattern is great for practising your stitches and joining in new colours, and you will be surprised how quickly the scarf grows. I have used a beautifully soft cotton-mix yarn, so even the most sensitive skins can wrap up snugly in this scarf.

The scarves

to make

Three-colour scarf

Garter st stripe sequence

Row 1: Knit using yarn A.

Row 2: Knit using yarn A.

Row 3: Knit using yarn B.

Row 4: Knit using yarn B.

Row 5: Knit using yarn C.

Row 6: Knit using yarn C.

Rep these 6 rows.

St-st stripe sequence

Row 1: Knit using yarn A.

Row 2: K2, P31, K2, using yarn A.

Work 8 more rows using yarn A.

Row 11: Knit using yarn B.

Row 12: K2, P31, K2, Knit using yarn B.

Work 8 more rows using yarn B.

Row 21: Knit using yarn C.

Row 22: K2, P31, K2, Knit using yarn C.

Work 8 more rows using yarn C.

Rep these 30 rows.

Using 5 mm (US 8) needles and yarn A, cast on 35 sts.

**Work 20 cm (8 in) of g-st stripe.

Work 30 cm (12 in) of st-st stripe.

Work 10 cm (4 in) of g-st stripe.

Work 10 cm (4 in) of st-st stripe.

Work 30 cm (12 in) of g-st stripe.

Work 10 cm (4 in) of st-st stripe.

Work 20 cm (8 in) of g-st stripe**.

Work 30 cm (12 in) of st-st stripe.

Work 20 cm (8 in) of g-st stripe, ending with a RS row.

Cast off knitwise.

Plain scarf

Using 5 mm (US 8) needles, cast on 35 sts.

Working in one colour only, work as for 3-colour Scarf from ** to **,

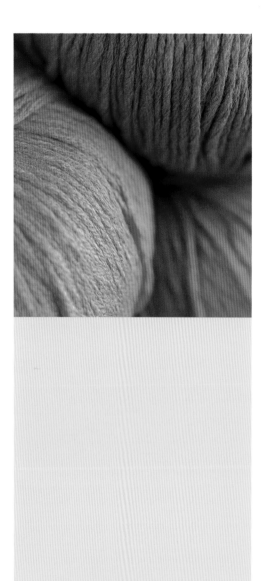

ending with a WS row. Cast off knitwise.

Four-colour scarf

Garter st stripe sequence

Row 1: Knit using yarn A.

Row 2: Knit using yarn A.

Row 3: Knit using yarn B.

Row 4: Knit using yarn B.

Row 5: Knit using yarn C.

Row 6: Knit using yarn C.

Row 7: Knit using yarn D.

Row 8: Knit using yarn D.

Rep these 8 rows.

St-st stripe sequence

Row 1: Knit using yarn A.

Row 2: K2, P25, K2, using yarn A.

Work 4 more rows using yarn A.

Row 7: Knit using yarn B.

Row 8: K2, P25, K2, using yarn B.

Work 4 more rows using yarn B.

Row 13: Knit using yarn C.

Row 14: K2, P25, K2, using yarn C.

Work 4 more rows using yarn C.

Row 19: Knit using yarn D.

Row 20: K2, P25, K2, using yarn D.

Work 4 more rows.

Rep these 26 rows.

Using 5 mm (US 8) knitting needles and yarn A, work picot cast-on as folls:

Cast on 20 sts, cast off 20 sts, 1 st on LH needle, *cast on 24 sts, cast off 20 sts* (5 sts on LH needle), work from * to * 6 times more. (29 sts)

Working 4-colour stripe sequences, work as for 3-colour Scarf from ** to **, ending with a RS row.

Work picot cast-off as folls:

Next row (WS): K1, turn and *cast on 20 sts, cast off 24 sts knitwise*, work from * to * until all sts are cast off.

Useful information

UK and US knitting terminology

Most terms used in UK and US knitting patterns are the same, but a few are different. The most common differences are listed here:

UK	US
cast off	bind off
moss stitch	seed stitch
stocking stitch	stockinette stitch
tension	gauge
yarn over needle	yarn over (yo)
yarn forward	yarn over (yo)
yarn round needle	yarn over (yo)

Knitting needle conversion chart

This chart shows you how the different knitting needle-size systems compare.

Metric	US sizes	Old UK
2 mm	0	14
2^1/4mm	1	13
2^3/4 mm	2	12
3 mm		11
3^1/4 mm	3	10
3^3/4 mm	5	9
4 mm	6	8
4^1/2 mm	7	7
5 mm	8	6
5^1/2 mm	9	5
6 mm	10	4
6^1/2 mm	10^1/2	3
7 mm	10^1/2	2
7^1/2 mm	11	1
8 mm	11	0
9 mm	13	00
10 mm	15	000

Index

V

W

Y

Acknowledgements

Executive Editors: Sarah Tomley and Katy Denny
Editor: Kate Tuckett
Pattern Checker: Pauline Hornsby
Executive Art Editor and Desginer: Joanna MacGregor
Photographer: Vanessa Davies
Illustrator: Kuo Kang Chen
Senior Production Controller: Manjit Sihra

Author biography

Louisa Harding studied Fashion Textiles at Brighton University, UK. A placement at Rowan Yarns resulted in the publication of two of her early designs in the Rowan Magazines. After graduation, she travelled to Canada to assist a hand-knit designer in setting up her ready-to-wear collection. On her return, Louisa became an in-house designer for Rowan Yarns, ultimately becoming the designer and brand co-ordinator for Jaeger Handknits. She now works as a freelance designer.